CLOSER TO JESUS

Closer to Jesus

Michael Green

Hodder & Stoughton
LONDON SYDNEY AUCKLAND

Copyright © Michael Green

First published in Great Britain 1995

The right of Michael Green to be identified as the Author of
the Work has been asserted by him in accordance with the
Copyright, Designs and Patents Act 1988.

Compiled by Ricarda Leask

Full acknowledgments are at the end of this book

10 9 8 7 6 5 4 3 2 1

British Library Cataloguing in Publication Data
A record for this book is available from the British Library

ISBN 0 340 64217 3

Typeset by Hewer Text Composition Services, Edinburgh
Printed and bound in Great Britain by
Cox & Wyman, Reading, Berks

Hodder and Stoughton Ltd
A Division of Hodder Headline PLC
338 Euston Road
London NW1 3BH

Contents

Preface   7

1 Checking the foundations   9
2 Turning the pain around   12
3 Following the instructions   17
4 Tackling temptation   20
5 Paying the price   25
6 Making us like Jesus   29
7 Recognising radiance   33
8 Judging by appearances   37
9 Sacrificing everything   40
10 Holding to humility   43
11 Manifesting miracles   46
12 Soothing the pain   51
13 Dealing with doubting   56
14 Stooping very low   61
15 Hoping for heaven   64
16 Making all things new   67
17 Copying the Master   71
18 Breaking down the barriers   75
19 Conquering everything   79
20 Dismantling the divisions   83
21 Changing direction   88
22 Substituting goodness   91
23 Overcoming evil   95
24 Practising perfection   99
25 Seeking little children   101

26 Giving rest to the weary   107
27 Living in the Bible   111
28 Taking Communion   115
29 Encountering Christ   119
30 Lighting up the darkness   123

Acknowledgments   128

Preface

The purpose of *20 Minutes with God* is to give you an opportunity to reflect on different aspects of the life of Jesus and to discover more of their significance for you today.

To get the most from it, you will need to have ready a Bible and a pen. Some of the reflections take the form of questions to answer, while others are more meditative: in many cases space has been allowed for you to record your responses, thoughts, feelings – or even questions of your own that may be prompted by the readings.

Some of the chapters end with a *For further study* section. These are optional; you could use them if you have more than twenty minutes available.

The reflections are designed for individuals, couples or groups meeting to pray or study together. Sharing your thoughts and responses to the reflections with others can be valuable, and sometimes it is suggested that you do this anyway, even if you are using the book on your own.

Before you begin each chapter, it would be a good idea to take a few minutes to be still, to try to lay aside the particular pressures or pleasures of your day, and to focus your mind and heart on God. You may like to use these words from Jesus to help quieten your heart and prepare to learn from him:

> *Come to me, all you who are weary and burdened, and I will give you rest. Take my yoke upon you and learn*

from me, for I am gentle and humble in heart, and you will find rest for your souls. For my yoke is easy and my burden is light.

Matthew 11: 28–30

1

Checking the foundations

Reading: Matthew 7:24–29

'Everyone who hears these words of mine and puts them into practice is like a wise man who built his house on the rock. The rain came down, the streams rose, and the winds blew and beat against that house; yet it did not fall, because it had its foundation on the rock. But everyone who hears these words of mine and does not put them into practice is like a foolish man who built his house on sand. The rain came down, the streams rose, and the winds blew and beat against that house, and it fell with a great crash.'

When Jesus had finished saying these things, the crowds were amazed at his teaching, because he taught as one who had authority, and not as their teachers of the law.

Jesus' teaching was memorable. Nobody had ever taught like this before, nor have they since. It was so vivid and memorable. It was so powerfully authoritative – 'Truly, truly I tell you . . .' Who was this 'I'? He taught them, says Mark, as one who had authority, and not as the scribes (the clergy of the day). The content of his teaching was no less staggering. He taught that the long-awaited kingdom of God had actually arrived with himself! He invited those who were weary and heavy laden to come to himself. He said that he would satisfy those with deep inner thirst. He told them that there was nothing they could do to make themselves acceptable to God.

On the contrary, God had done all that was necessary. He was like a king who forgave his debtor an incalculable debt simply out of the kindness of his heart. He was like a nobleman who threw a great wedding party for his son, to which he invited not only friends and relations but the scum off the city streets. God is like that. And, said Jesus, he is not merely that generous, but he is sensitive to how people feel when confronted with great generosity. So he provides not only the wedding reception free, gratis and for nothing; but also the clothes for people coming in to wear, so that all are the same and none need be embarrassed at his rags, and none can be proud of his finery.

'No man ever spoke like this man!' said the soldiers who had been sent to arrest him, when they returned without having accomplished their task. And they were right. There has been no parallel in the history of the world to the quality, the power and the authority of the teaching of Jesus. Nobody has been able to show any evil contained within it. Nobody has been able to show any good that is not contained, explicitly or implicitly, within it. Nobody has been able to surpass it. People were amazed at it. 'How does this man know so much, never having been to university?' they asked. Jesus' answer was simple and devastating: 'My teaching is not mine but his that sent me. If any man is willing to do his will, he will have no doubts about where the teaching comes from – whether I speak from God or whether I speak from myself.' If you are still in doubt, take a slow read through the Sermon on the Mount in Matthew 5–7. And spend time reflecting on the closing verses and their implications.

Reflection

Look through the Sermon on the Mount (Matthew 5–7) and pick out ten precepts from the teaching of Jesus. Write them down. Now look at each one and think of specific ways in which it applies to you. Which do you find the most difficult to apply or to keep?

Jesus said that anyone who put his teaching into practice would be like someone building a house on a rock instead of on the sand. On what sort of foundation are you building your life? Ask God now to take a look with you at the quality of rock, rubble or sand on which you are building. Since it is so crucial to have a firm foundation, ask this master builder to expose the weaknesses, and to help you make them good.

For further study
Pick up a recent newspaper or magazine and look for examples of the precepts that you found being kept or ignored. What were the consequences of these actions?

2

Turning the pain around

Reading: Matthew 27:32–50

As they were going out, they met a man from Cyrene, named Simon, and they forced him to carry the cross. They came to a place called Golgotha (which means The Place of the Skull). There they offered him wine to drink, mixed with gall; but after tasting it, he refused to drink it. When they had crucified him, they divided up his clothes by casting lots. And sitting down, they kept watch over him there. Above his head they placed the written charge against him: THIS IS JESUS, THE KING OF THE JEWS. *Two robbers were crucified with him, one on his right and one on his left. Those who passed by hurled insults at him, shaking their heads and saying, 'You who are going to destroy the temple and build it in three days, save yourself! Come down from the cross, if you are the Son of God!'*

In the same way the chief priests, the teachers of the law and the elders mocked him. 'He saved others,' they said, 'but he can't save himself! He's the king of Israel! Let him come down now from the cross, and we will believe in him. He trusts in God. Let God rescue him now if he wants him, for he said, "I am the Son of God."' In the same way the robbers who were crucified with him also heaped insults on him.

From the sixth hour until the ninth hour darkness

*came over all the land. About the ninth hour Jesus cried
out in a loud voice, 'Eloi, Eloi, lama sabachthani?'
– which means, 'My God, my God, why have you
forsaken me?'*

*When some of those standing there heard this, they
said, 'He's calling Elijah.'*

*Immediately one of them ran and got a sponge. He
filled it with wine-vinegar, put it on a stick, and offered
it to Jesus to drink. But the rest said, 'Leave him alone.
Let's see if Elijah comes to save him.'*

*And when Jesus had cried out again in a loud voice,
he gave up his spirit.*

At some time or other in life, everybody has to suffer. It
is universal. Physical suffering, mental suffering, spiritual
suffering affect every household, and embrace every
nation and colour and creed. The problem of suffering
is the greatest stumbling-block for many to believing
in a good and loving God. What has Christianity to
say to this most pressing cry of the human heart in
anguish 'Why should this happen to me?'? God has
given us the cross of Christ *non ut dicamus sed ne
sileamus*. It is not the final and complete explication
of the problem of pain, but it does shed a blazing patch
of light upon it. A chapter like Matthew 27, depicting
Jesus on his cross, enables us to see a number of positive
factors even in the midst of outrageous suffering and
injustices.

First, the crucifixion of Jesus shows that there can
be a fellowship in suffering. God does not torment us
and leave us on our own. He may not have given full
explanation of pain, but he has come to share it. God

is a suffering God. He does not stay immune from the anguish of his creatures. It breaks his heart. The cross of Christ means we can never say to God 'You don't care' or 'You don't understand.' He is in there with us. There is no suffering we can bear which he does not know from the inside. There is no injustice we can suffer which he does not comprehend from personal experience. And in times of greatest suffering it is not explanation we need so much as companionship. That God has provided for us in the sufferings of Jesus, and in his risen presence.

Second, we see from Calvary that there is a value in suffering. It is not fruitless and in vain. For much of our suffering Hebrews 12:11 holds true: 'For the moment all suffering seems painful rather than pleasant; later it yields the peaceful fruit of righteousness to those who have been trained by it.' Certainly the cross of Jesus has been incalculably fruitful. He has seen the fruit of the travail of his soul – and been satisfied (Isaiah 53:11). There is always value to be found somewhere in suffering, though it is usually only afterwards that this becomes apparent.

Third, peace is possible in suffering. Even in the paroxysm of death Jesus maintained a peace which enabled him to hand over his spirit to his Father (Matthew 27:50). His example was not lost on Peter. 'Therefore let those who suffer according to God's will do right and entrust their souls to a faithful Creator' (1 Peter 4:19). In the midst of anguish and desolation, there is a rock beneath. God knows what we can bear, and will temper our trials to enable us to endure them in peace, the peace to which Christ showed the way.

Fourth, there may be healing in suffering. In a strange passage in Matthew 8:17 the evangelist makes a secondary application of the Suffering Servant motif of Isaiah 53 to the healings of Jesus. He maintains that 'He took our infirmities and bore our diseases.' Many who have suffered the horror of being neglected from the earliest days of their life, many who have been seared by the most terrible inner hurts, have found healing at the cross of Jesus when they understood what he endured for them of desolation and rejection.

Fifth, there is an outcome to suffering. For the Christian the cross can never be separated from the resurrection. And the resurrection speaks of God's triumph over suffering. Jesus drained the cup of suffering to the dregs, and it failed to poison him, or embitter him, or make him distrust his Father. Accordingly, Good Friday was followed by Easter Day. Suffering, if this world were all, would be inexplicable and unjustifiable. But this world is not all there is. What is sown in tears will be reaped in joy. It was so for Jesus. It will be so for his suffering followers.

The cross empty of Jesus, therefore, has much to say to the sufferer. We should not be surprised when suffering strikes, nor expect to be exempt from it. We should allow it to draw us closer to the crucified Jesus. If we suffer with him we shall also reign with him. No tears fall unnoticed on the ground of Calvary.

Reflection

'There is no suffering we can bear which he does not know from the inside.' What does 'suffering' mean to you? Your own pain? Someone else's? Write down some of the words or phrases that come into your mind. Then write down the feelings that accompany these things. Look back over the Bible passage and see where Jesus suffered the same things, or may have felt the same feelings.

'There is always value to be found somewhere in suffering.' What positive things have come out of your times of suffering?

For further study
How could you explain the significance of Christ's suffering to a suffering agnostic?

3

Following the instructions

Reading: Mark 12:28–31

One of the teachers of the law came and heard them debating. Noticing that Jesus had given them a good answer, he asked him, 'Of all the commandments, which is the most important?'

'The most important one,' answered Jesus, 'is this: "Hear, O Israel, the Lord our God, the Lord is one. Love the Lord your God with all your heart and with all your soul and with all your mind and with all your strength." The second is this: "Love your neighbour as yourself." There is no commandment greater than these.'

You and I can't get to heaven on our own good deeds, for the simple reason that they are not good enough for God.

'What?' you say. 'I'm a good-living type. I've kept the Ten Commandments.' Have you? I wonder. Have you kept the first commandment of all, to give God number one place in your life? I haven't. Jesus said it meant loving the Lord our God with all our heart and mind and soul and strength. I simply haven't begun to keep that first and greatest commandment. I break it every day. And that is not a very encouraging start as I set out to establish myself before God as the fine one who does their best and can't be expected to do more.

I glance down the other commandments. I must not make my own image of God? Well, I don't make graven images, of course. But I do tend to say 'I can't believe in a God who . . .' or 'The God I believe in is like this . . .' I make him in my image, rather than stopping to find out what he has revealed himself to be in the Bible.

I must not take the name of God in vain? I do it every day without thinking. Keeping the Sabbath day holy, one day in seven separate for God and family and rest? Don't make me laugh. Honour father and mother? Not likely. When I'm young I rebel against them as hard as I can. When I'm married I neglect them. When they are old I stuff them in an old people's home. Honour them indeed!

I feel a bit better seeing the command not to kill. I have never done that. But hang on a minute: didn't Jesus say something about the one who hates being just as repulsive to God as the one who gives vent to hatred in murder?

It's the same with that command about adultery. I may not have gone in for the wife-swapping parties that some of my friends indulge in. But how about that dance when I went a lot further than I intended? How about the lustful thoughts that jostle through my mind whenever I see a shapely woman? Yes, Jesus was right when he put those thoughts down to just the same weakness in human nature as produces adultery.

'Thou shalt not steal.' But I'm afraid I do. Steal goods from the shops, when nobody is looking; steal a free ride from the bus, when the conductor doesn't notice; steal from the tax man by getting paid in cash not by cheque; yes, it happens. And as for not bearing false witness against my neighbour, why, that's what sells the Sunday papers. A little bit of scandal, a bit of exaggeration, of character assassination, of making myself look big in comparison. That final command against coveting, against unrestrained desire for what is not mine – why the whole of our society is built on covetousness! You covet the neighbour's car and partner and washing machine and freezer and colour TV and . . . Don't be stupid; life is built on coveting. OK then, but don't turn round and tell me that you have kept the Ten Commandments and are therefore a splendid person whom God ought to be proud to know. You have broken the lot. And so have I.

Reflection

Read Jesus' words in the Bible passage again, as if he were saying them directly to you. What does it mean to love him with all your heart? With all your soul? With all your mind? With all your strength?

And what does it mean to love your neighbour as yourself?

How do you feel about all these commandments?

Turn your thoughts and feelings into prayer to the God who loves you so much more than you love him.

4

Tackling temptation

Reading: Matthew 4:1–11

Then Jesus was led by the Spirit into the desert to be tempted by the devil. After fasting forty days and forty nights, he was hungry. The tempter came to him and said, 'If you are the Son of God, tell these stones to become bread.'

Jesus answered, 'It is written: "Man does not live on bread alone, but on every word that comes from the mouth of God."'

Then the devil took him to the holy city and made him stand on the highest point of the temple. 'If you are the Son of God,' he said, 'throw yourself down. For it is written:

"He will command his angels concerning you, and they will lift you up in their hands, so that you will not strike your foot against a stone."'

Jesus answered him, 'It is also written: "Do not put the Lord your God to the test."'

Again, the devil took him to a very high mountain and showed him all the kingdoms of the world and their splendour. 'All this I will give you,' he said, 'if you will bow down and worship me.'

Jesus said to him, 'Away from me, Satan! For it is written: 'Worship the Lord your God, and serve him only.''

Then the devil left him, and angels came and attended him.

Why does God allow temptation? That is a question Christians often ask. Well, he allowed it for Jesus. And after a high spiritual experience, such as the baptism undoubtedly was for Jesus, temptation frequently comes, and properly comes. It sorts out the emotional 'high' from the reality of spiritual conquest and growth. We are not meant to live on the 'junk foods' of spiritual highs. We are meant to live on that bread which comes from God alone, even if it is bread in the desert. Temptation is deliberately allowed by God. Its arrival does not mean that God's blessing has evaporated. It simply allows the ephemeral and the emotional to be separated from the lasting. Temptation builds spiritual muscle.

It would be a great mistake to suppose that the story of the temptations are included in the Gospel primarily to provide an example to Christian disciples, though they do provide that example. These temptations were messianic. They were uniquely appropriate to God's Son, who had just received a very clear vision of his mission. How was he to carry it out? How was he to lead people back to God? Was he to adopt the path of the conquering King or of the suffering Servant?

The rabbis had all sorts of expectations about the messianic kingdom. One of them ran like this. 'When King Messiah comes, he will stand upon the roof of the holy place. Then he will announce to Israel "Ye poor, the time of your redemption draws nigh."' The rabbis were also clear that when Messiah came there would be a repetition of the gift of manna in the desert. That is

why the Jews got so excited in John chapter 6 when Jesus
fed the multitude in a desert place. That is why they tried
to make him king. They knew their Scriptures, and the
writings of their rabbis. They knew that when manna in
the wilderness came, that would be the sign of the kingdom
breaking in.

What temptations to bypass the cross, to short-circuit
the path of obedience, and adopt the role of the Son and
the King without stooping to the role of the suffering
Servant! That was the particular thrust of the third temptation. To gain universal dominion back from the usurper
Prince, but to do so by striking a bargain with him rather
than striking him through the heart with the wood of the
cross. To be sure, the temptations to be selfish, to opt for
the sensational and to compromise, come the way of all
Christians, but they are recorded here so that we may see
the testing of God's Son. Is his messiahship to be the slave
of popular expectation? Or will he go to the cross to win
the crown?

Adam had failed. Adam had tempted God: he had
idolatrously gone for the tree in the midst of the garden
when he had been told not to. Adam had disobeyed God,
when he knew he was God's Son. Adam had grabbed at
sensual satisfaction because of the hunger of his body. And
the last Adam won where the first Adam fell. Here is the
recapitulation of history. Jesus succeeded where Adam
had failed.

Moreover, Jesus succeeded where Israel had failed.
The background to this story lies in Deuteronomy 8:1–5,
from which Jesus quotes in his first reply to Satan.
Moses recalls how God led the Israelites in the desert
forty years 'to humble you and to test you in order to
know what was in your heart, whether or not you would
keep his commands'. And Israel failed comprehensively.
They tempted God at Meribah and Massah. They were
idolatrous with the golden calf. They grabbed at manna in
the wilderness. Jesus, the fulfilment of Israel, succeeded
where Israel, in its historical manifestation, had failed.

Notice how Jesus overcame these temptations. 'It is written . . . it is written . . . it is written . . .' The quotations come from Deuteronomy 8:3, 6:13, 6:16. They suggest that Jesus had been reading Deuteronomy in his own devotional reading. From within these two chapters he draws on material that he has learnt. And the Spirit, which came upon him so powerfully at his baptism, was able to take the Scriptures that he had learnt and use them in spiritual warfare. 'The sword of the Spirit is the word of God' (Ephesians 6:17), and if we do not know our way about the Scriptures and do not trust the Spirit in warfare against Satan we will not share in the victory of God's Son. But if we do, the Spirit will bring them to our attention at times when temptation presses; and, like Jesus, we shall have the power to overcome.

Reflection

What does 'temptation' mean to you personally? Write down some words and phrases.

What exactly was the temptation that Jesus faced? What was the real attraction of it all? How did Jesus resist it? What principles can you learn from the way Jesus responded that you can apply for yourself?

Look back over the past week, and see if you can identify the temptations you have faced. How have you responded? What has influenced your response? As occasions come to mind, pray appropriately – with gratitude to God for the times you found strength to resist, or with repentance for the times you caved in. Don't wallow in a sense of failure, but receive God's forgiveness and ask for grace to recognise and resist temptation this week.

5

Paying the price

Reading: Matthew 18:21–35

Then Peter came to Jesus and asked, 'Lord, how many times shall I forgive my brother when he sins against me? Up to seven times?'

Jesus answered, 'I tell you, not seven times, but seventy-seven times.

'Therefore, the kingdom of heaven is like a king who wanted to settle accounts with his servants. As he began the settlement, a man who owed him ten thousand talents was brought to him. Since he was not able to pay, the master ordered that he and his wife and his children and all that he had be sold to repay the debt.

'The servant fell on his knees before him. "Be patient with me," he begged, "and I will pay back everything." The servant's master took pity on him, cancelled the debt and let him go.

'But when that servant went out, he found one of his fellow servants who owed him a hundred denarii. He grabbed him and began to choke him. "Pay back what you owe me!" he demanded.

'His fellow servant fell to his knees and begged him, "Be patient with me, and I will pay you back."

'But he refused. Instead, he went off and had the man thrown into prison until he could pay the debt. When the other servants saw what had happened, they were greatly

distressed and went and told their master everything that had happened.

'Then the master called the servant in. "You wicked servant," he said, "I cancelled all that debt of yours because you begged me to. Shouldn't you have had mercy on your fellow servant just as I had on you?" In anger his master turned him over to the jailers until he should pay back all he owed.*

'This is how my heavenly Father will treat each of you unless you forgive your brother from your heart.'

I remember Bishop Stephen Neill, a Christian deeply versed in other faiths, describing the uniqueness of Christian forgiveness with moving simplicity. He explained how in Hinduism the principle of *karma* prevails everywhere: the Hindu doctrine of retribution. Your actions incur indebtedness in a multitude of ways. These debts have to be worked off in a further reincarnation. If you do well, your next life will be on a higher level. If not, it will be on a lower level. But always *karma* drives you on. There is no possibility of forgiveness. Indeed, it would be immoral, for you must pay your debts. The iron hand of *karma* rules all. The ethical structure of the world is parallel to the physical. The law of *karma* is as omnipresent as the law of gravity. And it says to the Hindu 'You sin . . . and you pay.'

What a contrast Christianity presents! Grace instead of retribution. Forgiveness instead of endless working-off of debts. Eternal life instead of countless reincarnations culminating in a sea of non-being. Because of what Christ did on Calvary the message of God to the believer is totally different from the Hindu concept. It says 'You sin . . . and I pay.'

That makes no sense in commerce: it makes excellent

sense in personal relationships. It happens every time we forgive.

How do I know that God is like this? Calvary is the answer. It shows what God has been like from the beginning. It is the effective symbol in time of what God eternally is. The cross shows the cost of forgiveness to God. It cost him no less than crucifixion to forgive us and to have us back in his family.

Forgiveness is costly to give. It is humbling to receive. So the wronged party who offers forgiveness often needs to stand alongside the one who has done the wrong, and help that person to a fresh start. The wronged party will take the one who has offended as a friend. It is in this context that the word *hetairos* is significant in the Gospels. It means 'friend' – almost 'old fellow'. Three times Jesus speaks of someone thus. In each case the words come from the injured party to the one who has done the wrong. Once it is said by the owner of the vineyard, reproached by one of the men who had worked for the whole day when he gave a full day's wage to those who had only worked the last hour. 'Friend,' said the owner, 'I am doing you no wrong. Did you not agree with me for a denarius? Do you begrudge my generosity?'

Once it is said by the king to the man who had barged into the wedding feast in his own clothes and had refused the proffered wedding garment. 'Friend, how did you get in here without a wedding garment?' And the man was speechless, because he had rejected free grace, and had regarded his own garments as good enough. And the third occasion is full of pathos. Jesus says to Judas, Judas who has come to betray him, 'Friend, why are you here?' Grace, forgiveness, are making their final bid for the heart of Judas, but in vain.

If God forgives, he must be a suffering God. Christians have often got confused at this point with the impassibility of God. *Paschō*, to suffer, can be used in two senses. One is simply 'to suffer'. That God has always been doing, bound up as he is with suffering humanity. And he reached the nadir of suffering on the cross. The other sense of *paschō* means 'to have something done to you without your consent'. In this sense God is impassible. But suffer he does, and he must. For love makes you vulnerable. And this is what makes the cross of Jesus credible.

To be sure, then, the category of law is not broad enough to embrace the cross of Christ, but it is an essential aspect of that cross. Forgiveness, however, operates in a different world from law, the world of personal relationships.

Reflection

'You sin . . . I pay.' Spend a few moments thinking about the enormity of God's message of forgiveness. Why should God pay for us? And if he is always going to bail us out, why shouldn't we go on sinning?

Recall some of the occasions when you have received God's forgiveness, and some occasions when you have been forgiven by other people. Which do you find easier to accept? Why?

Think of your own personal relationships. Is there anyone who needs your forgiveness now? What makes it hard for you to give it? What would enable you 'to stand alongside the one who has done the wrong and help that person to a new start'?

For further study
Can you think of reasons which could make the law of *karma* seem easier to accept than the concept of God's grace? How could you respond to them?

6

Making us like Jesus

Reading: 1 Corinthians 13:1–10

If I speak in the tongues of men and of angels, but have not love, I am only a resounding gong or a clanging cymbal. If I have the gift of prophecy and can fathom all mysteries and all knowledge, and if I have a faith that can move mountains, but have not love, I am nothing. If I give all I possess to the poor and surrender my body to the flames, but have not love, I gain nothing.

Love is patient, love is kind. It does not envy, it does not boast, it is not proud. It is not rude, it is not self-seeking, it is not easily angered, it keeps no record of wrongs. Love does not delight in evil but rejoices with the truth. It always protects, always trusts, always hopes, always perseveres.

Love never fails. But where there are prophecies, they will cease; where there are tongues, they will be stilled; where there is knowledge, it will pass away. For we know in part and we prophesy in part, but when perfection comes, the imperfect disappears.

There is real danger in prizing, let us say, speaking in tongues (which I believe can be a real gift of the Holy Spirit) so highly that those who lack it are regarded as second-class Christians if Christians at all. So far as we know, Jesus never spoke in tongues. And the Spirit is the Spirit of Jesus. It cannot, therefore, be a *Christian* insight to urge that speaking in tongues is an indispensable mark of life in the Spirit of Christ; whereas it is an undeniably Christian insight to insist that love and holiness, so manifest in the life of the incarnate One, should mark those who claim to have his Spirit. In a word, the Spirit of Jesus points us back to Jesus. If we want to understand and possess the Spirit in his fullness, we need to keep our eyes firmly on Christ himself, for it is to him that all the Spirit's authentic witness is directed. If we do this we shall not claim as the teaching of the Spirit what does not relate to Jesus. And we shall not claim as experience of the Spirit what cannot be shown to flow from Jesus.

There is a further sense in which the very strong link between the Spirit and Jesus will determine our experience of the Spirit. The Spirit of Jesus is the Spirit which marked him out as Son of God, as Servant of Yahweh, and sent him on his mission to Israel and the world. If the Spirit of Jesus is the gift bestowed on his followers, we shall expect to find the same characteristics marking authentic Christian life in the Spirit. And that is very much what we do find in the pages of the New Testament.

Take first the question of inheritance. Now there is a very obvious difference between us and Jesus. He was born by the express agency of the Holy Spirit; we are not. He was Son of God by right: we are sons and daughters only by adoption. Nevertheless it was the possession of the Spirit that set Jesus apart as the messianic Son of God, and brought the voice from heaven at his baptism 'Thou art my Son.' As Son, Jesus coined a new word for God. He called him 'Abba.' Nowhere in pre-Christian literature does anyone dare to call God by this intimate, family word which could better be translated as 'Daddy' or 'Dear Father'. It was a word for the intimacies of the family, not for the worship of God.

Jesus, the one set apart by the Spirit as *the* Son of God, dares to call God by this name. He alone has the right to, for he alone enjoys the intimate relation of sonship with God the Father. And it is into this relationship that he installs us. He enables us to pray the Lord's Prayer, which, in the form known to Luke, begins simply 'Abba', 'Father'. It is the Spirit who adopts us alongside Christ into this relationship with God, and who enables us to cry the 'Abba' of little children in the family of God. 'You have received the Spirit which makes you sons and daughters,' exults the Apostle Paul. 'When we cry "Abba! Father", it is the Spirit himself bearing witness with our Spirit that we are children of God, and if children then heirs, heirs of God and fellow-heirs with Christ, provided we suffer with him in order that we may also be glorified with him' (Romans 8:15ff). That is the incredible privilege and status of the Christian. Christians possess the Spirit of God's Son, which makes us sons and daughters of God, and enables us to utter the family cry to God as 'Abba'. Well may we conclude that the whole of the good news is concentrated in that single word, Abba.

Reflection

What characteristics of Jesus should mark the lives of believers (see verses 4–7)? Write them down, and look prayerfully at the list. Without being unduly self-deprecating, look back over the last few days and ask yourself how your life has been marked by them. If you're feeling brave, you could ask a close friend or spouse to tell you. No one will score 100 per cent on this, so take some time to ask the Holy Spirit to go on working in your life to make you more like Jesus, and to strengthen you especially in the areas where you feel you are weakest.

Adults often do not like to be thought of as 'children' by their parents. How do you feel about being called a 'child' of God? How important to you is this aspect of your relationship with God? Why?

7

Recognising radiance

Reading: Psalm 19:1–8

The heavens declare the glory of God;
the skies proclaim the work of his hands.
Day after day they pour forth speech;
night after night they display knowledge.
There is no speech or language where their voice is
not heard.
Their voice goes out into all the earth,
their words to the ends of the world.

In the heavens he has pitched a tent for the sun,
which is like a bridegroom coming forth from his
pavilion,
like a champion rejoicing to run his course.
It rises at one end of the heavens
and makes its circuit to the other;
nothing is hidden from its heat.

The law of the LORD is perfect, reviving the soul.
The statutes of the LORD are trustworthy,
making wise the simple.
The precepts of the LORD are right,
giving joy to the heart.
The commands of the LORD are radiant,
giving light to the eyes.

When we stop to think of Jesus, the Jesus we profess to love and follow, the differences between the modern evangelist and the Master are so great as to make us wonder if we are on the same team. It is hardly an exaggeration to say that our understanding of truth has been propositional. But his understanding was personal. This emphasis on personal integrity and character is one of the great marks of truth as seen in the Old Testament, where truth, *emeth*, is already preparing us for the declaration, 'I am the Truth.' But we are bound into the classical mindset so clearly displayed by Pontius Pilate in his question, '*What* is truth?' The truth stood in front of him, and he could not see it. He was simply incapable of taking in the fact that final truth is not a matter of propositions but a quality of life. And it is here that we are so unlike Jesus. Our mindset has been that of Pilate. We have assumed that truth consists in doctrinal statements which can be packaged and need to be disseminated. Not so Jesus.

Jesus revelled in creation, the good creation of his heavenly Father. We Christians have not been notable for our care about the environment. The Green movement has not been led by Christians. We have so concentrated on redemption that we have failed to understand or revel in creation. The results are catastrophic: a false other-worldliness, a suspicion of the arts, a dichotomy between 'ordinary jobs' and 'full-time service', and acquiescence through a conspiracy of silence in the rape of the earth. We are only now beginning to repent of this attitude. But our repentance may yet prove to have begun too late. If any people ever had the chance to understand the interdependence of humanity and nature, the balance between our headship over creation and our servanthood and stewardship to God, then it was those who professed the Christian faith and lived by the Christian Bible. But we have failed.

Jesus was such a happy man. True, he was at times 'a man of sorrows and acquainted with grief', especially as the cross drew near. But the prevailing impact he makes in the Gospels is one of life and love and joy. That is what drew people so irresistibly to him. Joy is infectious. It has been well said that Christianity is more often caught than taught. But by our rationalism and formalism, by the absence of radiant and carefree celebration in our ranks, we have not had that magnetic impact which Jesus undoubtedly possessed. We have hidden him in doctrine and in churchianity. If people saw deep, unselfish joy in us Christians, they would be predisposed to listen when we explained where that joy comes from.

Jesus had profound empathy with people in their feelings. He wept at the tomb of Lazarus. We read that he was filled with compassion (literally 'he was moved in his guts') at the sight of helpless, purposeless people, lost and unaware of where they were heading. He felt so much for the lepers that he did the unthinkable, and touched them. He felt for that rich young ruler who loved his money more than Jesus. He really loved him. Jesus did not keep his feelings under lock and key. His empathy drew people to him. They felt that here was someone who cared, someone who understood. But, alas, that is not the universal impression of the Christian Church or the Christian evangelist. The Church is too formal, too busy with its programmes, to bother about the feelings and heart-cries of ordinary people. Evangelists are too preoccupied with their message, their delivery, their impact, to bother too much about the individual. If they do, in a 'time of ministry' after they have issued their challenge, that time will probably be short and perfunctory. We have ceased to feel the heartbeat of hurting people. We have ceased to care. At least, that is the impression we have managed to give. No wonder evangelism does not seem to be sharing good news, but the quest for new members.

Reflection

Write down ten good and beautiful things about the created world we live in, and then ten bad or ugly things about it. What has caused them? What are your thoughts and feelings as you look at the two lists? Use them to compose a prayer of appreciation for the world God created and of sorrow for what is happening to it.

How can you show the life and love and joy of Christ to other people? In what ways do you experience these qualities for yourself? How do they become submerged? How can they be nurtured?

And what about your church? When people come to it, do they find 'rationalism and formalism' or 'radiant and carefree celebration'? What is there of the empathy of Christ in the church?

As you consider these matters, ask God to direct your thinking, to encourage or rebuke you, and to lead you forward in his ways.

8

Judging by appearances

Reading: 1 Peter 3:3–4

Your beauty should not come from outward adornment, such as braided hair and the wearing of gold jewellery and fine clothes. Instead, it should be that of your inner self, the unfading beauty of a gentle and quiet spirit, which is of great worth in God's sight.

The Jesus who meets us in the pages of the four Gospels (the accounts of Jesus written by his friends) is very different from the picture many have of him. He is nothing like the 'gentle Jesus meek and mild' of the children's stories. He is not the miserable holy man who never laughs. He is not the fearsome judge who watches to see if we are enjoying ourselves and then tells us to stop. Nor is he the lifeless figure in the stained-glass window. Jesus, as the Gospels reveal him to us, is radiantly alive and supremely attractive.

There is a great deal we would love to know which we simply are not told. We do not even know what he looked like. He was a Palestinian Jew, and as such the colour of his skin would be olive, his eyes brown, and his nose hooked. Palestinian Jews had black hair, and usually wore it long and carefully groomed. They valued a full beard, and it appears on many of the coins of the day. His mother tongue was Aramaic, a dialect of Hebrew, which he would have spoken with a northern accent common to Galilee where he was brought up. But he could speak some Greek and possibly Latin, and was thoroughly at home in the Hebrew scriptures. He wore a sleeveless undergarment with a girdle, the customary cloak and sandals, and carried a staff on journeys. That is all we know about his appearance, or can guess with confidence.

But the Gospels have no interest in these things. They are profoundly disinterested in his size, the colour of his eyes and hair, and even his age and strength. These external things are unimportant. What someone is like stems from their character. And here the Gospels are eloquent.

The first thing that strikes me is that Jesus was such delightful company. People walked miles to be with him. And they were folk from widely different backgrounds who normally would have had nothing in common. Judges and soldiers, fishermen and prostitutes, all found his company irresistible. He cheerfully broke the taboos which kept people apart in Judaism's highly structured society. He mixed with top people and street people with equal ease. He was at home in the tavern just as he was in the temple. He could win the adoration of the crowd, yet loved solitary and simple settings. He was an inspiration to the uneducated and intellectuals alike. Although himself a carpenter, devoid of theological training, he could attract and teach a man like Nicodemus who had the highest theological training and social privileges in the nation. He could also offer an entirely new life to a wildly immoral woman from a hostile neighbouring country. Indeed, women were welcomed as an important part of his movement: he respected them, and they were devoted to him. This was most remarkable in a culture where the pious Jew thanked God daily that he was not born a woman. Jesus was sometimes to be found surrounded by little children, jumping delightedly upon his knee. He held them up as examples to grown men and women, whereas normal religious leaders were too solemn and self-important to view them as anything but an intrusion. Jesus was a man for all types. He was marvellous company.

Reflection

How would you describe Jesus Christ to someone who knew nothing about him? Write down some aspects of his personality.

How important to you are external appearances – both your own and other people's? How important do you think they are to God?

For further study
What are the taboos, spoken or unspoken, that keep people apart in today's society? Does your experience of Christianity reinforce these taboos, or ignore them? (Think of your own church – is it somewhere that people from widely different backgrounds mix with ease, or do its members come from very similar backgrounds?)

9

Sacrificing everything

Reading: 1 John 4:9–11

This is how God showed his love among us: he sent his one and only Son into the world that we might live through him. This is love: not that we loved God, but that he loved us and sent his Son as an atoning sacrifice for our sins. Dear friends, since God so loved us, we also ought to love one another.

Jesus had predicted that if he was lifted up from the earth, he would draw all kinds of people to himself, and this has proved abundantly true. Until the cross of Jesus, the faith of his disciples was weak and vacillating. The cross, which might well have dashed to the ground such fragile faith as they had, in fact lit it into an inextinguishable blaze. Now that is a very remarkable thing. Remarkable to start believing in your leader once he is dead and gone. Remarkable to start believing that he is God's anointed rescuer once he has so signally failed to produce the goods and has ended in disgrace on a gibbet. Most remarkable of all when you remember that in the Old Testament it says that anyone exposed on a gibbet rests under the curse of God. Remarkable, but true. The Christian movement only took root once Jesus was crucified. The cross became the symbol of the new movement. The symbol of death and shame turned into the most glorious badge of discipleship. How did that happen?

It was as they saw him die that understanding began to dawn. The sheer self-sacrifice of it; the gentleness, the horror, the love, the pardon, the victory intertwined with that cross quickened their insight. Listen to Peter, who was there. He is writing years later to scattered Christians throughout Turkey and Southern Russia. 'He himself bore our sins in his body on the tree,' he exclaims. And a little later: 'Christ has once and for all suffered for sins, the just for the unjust, that he might bring us to God.' Peter had come to see that Jesus did indeed die in the place of cursing, that awesome gibbet: but that the curse was ours and not his own. He did indeed bear sins: but they were our sins, not his own, for he had none.

It is astonishing that through this squalid murder on Calvary the followers of Jesus should have received such lasting assurance about who he was. But such is the case. Mark tells us of the death of Jesus and then immediately goes on, 'And the curtain of the temple was torn in two, from top to bottom.' That curtain was there to keep people out from the presence of God, manifested in the holy of holies. When the curtain was split wide open, at the death of Jesus, it was a symbolic gesture to show that the way into God's presence had been opened for all. And immediately we find a Gentile soldier, who had personally killed this same Jesus, going, so to speak, through that split curtain into God's presence with the awed confession on his lips: 'Truly this man was the Son of God.'

The author of Hebrews cannot affirm the full deity of Jesus without continuing, 'When he had made purification for sins, he sat down at the right hand of the Majesty on high.' And Paul was no less clear that in the cross he saw God Almighty dealing with the basic human problem, sin.

'In Christ God was reconciling the world to himself, not counting their trespasses against them.' That is precisely what Jesus himself had said he would do. Three times in Mark's Gospel he predicted his passion, and then capped it with the explanation: 'The Son of man . . . came . . . to give his life as a ransom for many.' It was in that supreme act of self-sacrifice and sin-bearing that the disciples saw straight through to the heart of God. God had come to them in Christ, and God had saved them through his cross.

Reflection

'It was in that supreme act of self-sacrifice and sin-bearing that the disciples saw straight through to the very heart of God.' What attributes of God are revealed through the death of Jesus? What impact do they have on your own life? What does this supreme sacrifice of Jesus have to say about the way you live and love?

What does the cross mean to you personally? Write down words and phrases, or draw pictures to express your thoughts and feelings about it. Try to avoid theological jargon, and use them as a springboard for prayer.

For further study
Using a concordance, look through the New Testament and find the different ways that the writers use to describe the purpose and effect of the death of Jesus.

10

Holding to humility

Reading: Matthew 18:1–4

At that time the disciples came to Jesus and asked, 'Who is the greatest in the kingdom of heaven?'

He called a little child and had him stand among them. And he said: 'I tell you the truth, unless you change and become like little children, you will never enter the kingdom of heaven. Therefore, whoever humbles himself like this child is the greatest in the kingdom of heaven. And whoever welcomes a little child like this in my name welcomes me.'

If we were to stop and think what was most important in church relationships, I do not think many Christians would come up with this quality which Jesus wants to see as the first and foremost characteristic of his disciples – humility. 'Who is the greatest in the kingdom?' ask the disciples. Alas, Christians ancient and modern are often preoccupied with that question. And, in sharp contrast to the disciples' fascination with status and position, Jesus takes a child – and they were of little account in antiquity

– puts him on his lap, and declares that greatness is to be
found precisely there. Real greatness is not to be found
in seeking to be praised and served by others, but in
seeking others to serve, especially those who have no
rights. Significantly, the first mark of Christians in the
church is the supreme mark of Jesus himself, humility.
If the Son of Man goes humbly as it is written of him, how
much more should his followers?

We can be fairly sure that when Jesus called the little
lad to him, he came promptly, and he stayed where he was
put. That child was accounted great by Jesus. Is that not a
clue to what real humility means? You come when Jesus
calls you and you stay where Jesus puts you. So humility
is not a matter of suppressing your drive and hiding your
gifts. The humble person is quite unselfconscious about it
all, like the lad. He claims no right from others, or from his
Master. He follows where Jesus calls and he stays where
Jesus puts him. That is humility.

Archbishop William Temple unselfconsciously displayed
that humility in his own character. He said 'I have never
sought and never refused a position of greater respon-
sibility.' That shows how humility can quite naturally
accompany great positions of leadership. It is a quality
that is imperative among Christians. Others may need to
'keep face' because they have no ultimate security to fall
back on. Christians should never need this. They know
they are accepted in Christ. They should be willing and
able to take their masks off, lay no pretence to greatness,
and be utterly at the disposal of Jesus. The American
preacher S. D. Gordon, not himself highly educated,
once advised 'Get every qualification you can and then
use it for God.' The trouble is that those who are not
humble spend much of their lives hunting qualifications
for their own sake, hoping that they will give them the
status and self-esteem they crave. But no. God has already
given us the highest status in the world. We are his *paides*,
his 'children'. But in Greek (as in Aramaic) the word also
means 'servants'.

Reflection

Make a list of words and phrases which describe or illustrate *humility*. Think of some people whose lives demonstrate this quality. Then examine your own life to see how you personally do, or do not, demonstrate humility. Turn your findings into prayer.

'You come when Jesus calls you and you stay where Jesus puts you . . . That is humility.' What helps you to hear the call of Jesus? What makes it hard to hear him? Think back to occasions when you have heard his call and try to remember the circumstances of the experience. How did you hear him? How did you know that it was God speaking, and not your own desire? If you feel that you have never heard God's voice clearly, ask him to teach and enable you to listen and to hear. Talk to others as well, and discover some of the different ways that God uses to speak to us.

For further study
Using a concordance, look up instances in the Bible where people have heard the call of God. Notice the means God uses to speak, and the kinds and characteristics of people who heard him.

11

Manifesting miracles

Reading: John 2:1–11

On the third day a wedding took place at Cana in Galilee. Jesus' mother was there, and Jesus and his disciples had also been invited to the wedding. When the wine was gone, Jesus' mother said to him, 'They have no more wine.'

'Dear woman, why do you involve me?' Jesus replied, 'My time has not yet come.'

His mother said to the servants, 'Do whatever he tells you.'

Nearby stood six stone water jars, the kind used by the Jews for ceremonial washing, each holding from twenty to thirty gallons.

Jesus said to the servants, 'Fill the jars with water'; so they filled them to the brim.

Then he told them, 'Now draw some out and take it to the master of the banquet.'

They did so, and the master of the banquet tasted the water that had been turned into wine. He did not realise where it had come from, though the servants who had drawn the water knew. Then he called the bridegroom aside and said, 'Everyone brings out the choice wine first and then the cheaper wine after the guests have had too much to drink; but you have saved the best till now.'

This, the first of his miraculous signs, Jesus performed

in Cana of Galilee. He thus revealed his glory, and his
disciples put their faith in him.

You cannot disentangle Jesus from miracle. In the last
century people tried hard to so pare away at the Gospel
records that they left us with a non-supernatural Jesus,
meek and mild, and never doing anything out of the
ordinary. Schweitzer and Barth, however, at the beginning
of this century, showed that it cannot be done. At every
point in the story of Jesus, and in every strand of the
Gospel record, you stub your foot against miracles. The
miracles began at his conception and birth: he was God's
Son, according to Mark; God's Word and agent in creation
according to John; the full repository of the Godhead
according to Paul (while none the less being 'born of
a woman'); the one who came into the world without
the agency of a human father, according to Matthew
and Luke.

The miracles continue in his ministry: miracles of
knowledge, miracles of healing, miracles of exorcism,
miracles over nature, and even some miraculous cases
of raising people from the dead. Artlessly and naturally
they are interwoven with the whole account. So much were
they part of Jesus' self-disclosure that John chose seven of
them, called them 'signs' (i.e. pointers to who Jesus really
is) and built his Gospel around them. By giving an account
of each of them, together with an explanatory discourse,
he shows us what Jesus' real significance is, and what he
can do for men. The one who fed the five thousand can
certainly feed the hungry soul. The one who opened blind
eyes can do as much for men and women blinded by pride
and prejudice. The one who raised the dead can bring

new life to someone who is spiritually dead. The miracles were never done for selfish purposes. They were never to show off. They were evoked by Jesus' compassion for human need and they were intended to show that the long-awaited Messiah had indeed arrived, and also that Jesus was the liberator who could unlock the various shackles of mankind.

The miracles were so well attested that we find the opponents of Jesus unable to deny them, and forced to assign them to an evil power. 'Through the ruler of the demons he casts out the demons,' said the Pharisees. 'But how can the devil cast out the devil?' asked Jesus. 'In that case his control would collapse in ruins' – which is manifestly not the case. The interesting thing to note is that his opponents did not and could not deny the efficacy of Jesus' cures and exorcisms. In later years they said that he had learned magic in Egypt, and that he was crucified on the eve of Passover for having practised sorcery in Egypt. That was the official party line in the Jewish Mishnah. But so clear was the power of his miracles that we find Jewish people trying to make use of that power without yielding their lives to Jesus.

In the Acts of the Apostles we find some of these people attempting exorcism 'by the Jesus whom Paul proclaims'. We read, with a touch of amusement, that the man with the evil spirit flew at them shouting, 'Jesus I know, and Paul I know; but who are you?', overpowered them, and handled them so roughly that they ran out of the house stripped and battered! There are several prohibitions in later Jewish literature against healing in the name of Jesus: 'A man shall have no dealing with the heretics [i.e. Christians] nor be cured by them even for the sake of an hour of life.'

The miracles of Jesus are hard to deny. Of course they are all secondary to the great miracles of the incarnation and the resurrection, but they stand as mute though powerful indicators of who Jesus is. When they saw the miracle at Cana his disciples, we read, believed in Jesus.

The raising of Lazarus to life had the same effect: 'Many of the Jews who had come to visit Mary, and had seen what Jesus did, put their faith in him.' And on another occasion, when he was besieged by an angry crowd, furious because of his claim to be God's Son, he said, 'My deeds done in my Father's name are my credentials . . . I and the Father are one . . . If I am not acting as my Father would, do not believe me. But if I am, accept the evidence of my deeds, even if you do not believe me.' The miracles of Jesus bore powerful testimony to his person as Son of God. They still do.

Reflection

We have a tendency to ask for miracles as a way out of a tight spot, or when a situation seems hopeless. That can make God seem to be merely a kind of emergency service. So what is the purpose of miracles and why does God do them?

How does the belief that God can work miracles affect the way you pray? What may prevent you from asking God to do the seemingly impossible?

What is the one thing that you would most like God to do for you? Imagine asking Jesus face to face: how does he respond?

For further study
What could you say to someone who finds it hard to believe the miracles of Jesus?

12

Soothing the pain

Reading: Isaiah 46:3–4

*Listen to me . . . you whom I have upheld
  since you were conceived,
  and have carried since your birth.
Even to your old age and grey hairs
  I am he, I am he who will sustain you.
I have made you and I will carry you;
  I will sustain you and I will rescue you.*

In the light of the attractiveness of Jesus, it is hardly surprising that men and women flocked to him. Jesus was surrounded by crowds, presumably because they felt that in some way he held the key to community: he was a wonderful person to be with. Jesus met and transformed the loneliness of Zacchaeus, a man whose relationships had become frozen because of his pursuit of money and his ruthlessness in dealing with people. Jesus met and transformed the woman taken in adultery: unlike the religious leaders, he neither sought her out in her sin nor condemned her when she was brought before him.

He understood her. He cared about her. He knew the hurt she had suffered and the guilt she felt. It was not condemnation she needed, but acquittal. He offered her just that, together with the pointer towards a better life, and the power to achieve it.

Jesus met and transformed the impetuous Peter, making this mercurial man, dominated by his emotions, into a stable leader of Christ's new community, a rock on which he could build. Jesus met and transformed John the dreamer, making him a mystic and a visionary who became the apostle of love. Jesus met and transformed the household of Jairus in its disappointment, its grief and bereavement. He met and transformed beggars like Bartimaeus, prostitutes like Mary Magdalene, crooked businessmen like Matthew. In every case his approach was tailored to the individual. In every case he entered into the need and the hurt which had marred that person's life, and spoke his word of healing and renewal.

And that is the heart of effective evangelism. Not many people are brought to Christ via the route of the intellect, though some are. Vital though the intellect is, most people are won when they sense Christ coming to touch broken places and torn feelings in their lives. This may be at a point of perceived, long-standing need. Or it may be that only when some aspect of Jesus is seen does the person recognise how empty or needy he has been all along.

A great many people today have never experienced love without strings attached. They have been appreciated when they have performed in a certain way, or made certain achievements. But they have known nothing of being loved for themselves, warts and all, alike in success and in failure. The unconditional love of Jesus for all and sundry can surge like a flood into a heart like that.

A great many people have a tremendously low self-image. It has been inculcated in them by parents who have dominated them and have failed to praise and love them: instead, a critical attitude has surrounded their childhood and youth. They have been made to feel no good. And this happens to people who are great achievers just as much as it does to poor achievers. External accomplishments tell us nothing about the inner feelings of the person concerned. It is when people who feel so inadequate and unimportant see that Jesus rates them very differently that the skies begin to clear. If he valued them so highly that he came for them and died for them – why, they must be something very special after all! And that realisation brings new life to many who are dogged by this spectre of a low self-image.

A great many people are lonely. It matters not one whit whether they have many friends or few, whether they are the fortunate in society or at the bottom of the pile. 'Why am I so lonely when there are so many people here?', a plea scratched on a school desk, is the agonising question of many hearts. The answer, of course, lies in the friend who sticks closer than anybody, the one who will never leave us nor forsake us once he is welcomed into our life. That companionship of Jesus, risen from the dead, alive for evermore, is the ultimate answer to loneliness. Millions the world over have proved its staying-power: be they politicians at the centre of the action, invalids on their beds, or believers incarcerated in solitary confinement. It will be the image of Jesus the friend which attracts such people. They do not need to know the evidence for the resurrection. They need to see in other lives, and wonderingly to accept for themselves, the possibility that this living Jesus would be willing to accompany them personally.

A great many people feel defeated. Defeated by habits too strong to break, defeated by the past catching up with them, defeated by inherited defects in character. They had imagined that Christianity was for good people, who dressed nicely and went to church on Sundays, not for the likes of them. God forgive us that such an impression could ever have got abroad, but it has. They need to see that Jesus takes failures and makes them saints. They may see it in the reclaimed lives of some of their friends and acquaintances. They may become assured of it in the loving perseverance of the person who is trying to bring the good news to them – often in the face of their own opposition and acrimony. But it is when they feel within themselves that Jesus is willing to take failures like themselves on board that new hope is born, and new life begun.

I hope enough has been said to show that what really matters is that the healing hand of the great physician should be brought gently into touch with the emotions as well as with the mind of the person concerned. A great deal of our evangelism is a total failure because it does not touch the heart and show where the Saviour can reach the hidden fears and hurts which plague us human beings – all of us.

Reflection

What are the ways in which God has sustained you, carried you and rescued you? What areas of brokenness or torn feelings has he met and transformed? Allow him to sift through your memories so that you can see how deeply he has been involved in your life.

In what ways do you need him to touch your life now? Imagine meeting him face to face, like the people in the Gospels. What needs in you would he see? Be still before him; rest in the knowledge that he knows you, understands you and loves you unconditionally. Allow him to come close to you and to touch your pain, your emptiness, your fear: whatever need you may have.

'In every case his approach was tailored to the individual. In every case he entered into the need and the hurt which had marred that person's life, and spoke his word of healing and renewal.' Think of some people who have not known the healing word of Christ. Pray for them now, asking him to enter into the needs and hurts which mar their lives, and to speak his word of healing and renewal. What might you be able to do to become an instrument of God's healing?

13

Dealing with doubting

Reading: John 20:24–29

Now Thomas (called Didymus), one of the Twelve, was not with the disciples when Jesus came. When the other disciples told him that they had seen the Lord, he declared, 'Unless I see the nail marks in his hands and put my finger where the nails were, and put my hand into his side, I will not believe it.'

A week later his disciples were in the house again, and Thomas was with them. Though the doors were locked, Jesus came and stood among them, and said, 'Peace be with you!' Then he said to Thomas, 'Put your finger here; see my hands. Reach out your hand and put it into my side. Stop doubting and believe.'

Thomas answered, 'My Lord and my God!'

Then Jesus told him, 'Because you have seen me, you have believed; blessed are those who have not seen and yet have believed.'

I am constantly surprised to see arguments continuing to pass to and fro, seeking to prove or disprove the

existence of God. The whole procedure is quite inap-
propriate, because, although there are good reasons for
believing in a Supreme Being, personal existence can
neither be proved nor disproved: it must be encountered. And the only God known to the Bible is not
the First Cause or the Unmoved Mover discussed in
philosophical argument, but the living God who made
us, who cares for us, and who comes to meet us in Jesus
Christ. It is beside the point to argue for or against the
traditional 'proofs' for God's existence. The Bible never
uses them. It never argues about God's existence at all,
but always assumes him as the basis for all else. It
points, instead, to Jesus Christ, who claimed that he
was revealing God to us. 'No one knows the Son but
the Father, and no one knows the Father but the Son
and any one to whom the Son chooses to reveal him.
Come to me, all who labour and are heavy laden, and
I will give you rest' (Matthew 11:27ff). Claims like this
make the imagination boggle. They mean – if they can
be relied on – that behind this world there is a loving,
personal God who has created all there is. This God
cares for us so much, despite our waywardness and
rebellion, that he chose to come and share our world,
and to make known to us his nature and his will in
the only terms we intimately understand, the terms of
human life.

And what a life! A life that has influenced art, music,
culture and literature more than any other before or since.
A life which has inspired most of the ideals of modern
education, hospitals, social services, freedom, the trade
unions and the welfare state. A life which embodied every
virtue, and was free from all human vices. However you
look at it, the character of Jesus was unparalleled. He set
the highest standards for human conduct that any teacher
has ever set, and unlike any other teacher, he kept to those
standards.

Moreover, Jesus accepted as his due the worship thought
proper to God alone. Peter fell at his feet and said 'You

are the Christ, the Son of the living God.' Thomas, in the upper room, cried out 'My Lord and my God.' In both cases Jesus accepted this tribute quite naturally. He took it as his right.

Claims such as these are breathtaking. They would sound like the ravings of a lunatic, were it not for the character and moral teaching of the man who uttered them. But how did he propose to authenticate his claims? Not by miracles. He refused to work these to order. In any case, miracles could never compel belief: people would always find some alternative explanation. So Jesus made the whole of his credibility rest upon the resurrection.

A Ugandan friend of mine sees the implication clearly. 'For me, he is not a mere hero of history, like those who fought and died in two world wars. He is my God, in full power of deity.' That is what Paul meant when, apparently drawing on an even earlier formulation, he says this about Jesus. 'He was descended from David according to the flesh, and designated Son of God in power according to the Spirit of holiness by his resurrection from the dead, Jesus Christ our Lord' (Romans 1:3f). The most compelling argument for the existence of God, and the sort of God described in Scripture, is Jesus Christ. By his incarnation, his teaching, his death, and supremely by his resurrection, he has shown us what God is like. He has shown us that God is personal. He has shown us that God is holy. He has shown us that God is love. He has shown us that God forgives – at infinite personal cost. He has shown us, by the resurrection, that evil will not have the last word in God's universe. In the risen Christ we have the answer to our doubts about God.

Reflection

What is it that enables *you* to believe and declare Jesus your Lord and your God? What aspects of your faith do you find hard to believe? Jesus responded to Thomas' doubt by giving him the proof he asked for – he didn't condemn him for finding the resurrection incredible. If you are someone to whom faith does not come easily, then be honest before God now, tell him what you find difficult to believe, and ask him to help you. Talk to others, too: you may find that they have wrestled with just the same questions that you have.

How does the fact that God became one of us, in the person of Jesus, help you to relate to him?

For further study
What exactly does the life, death and resurrection of Jesus tell us about the existence and the nature of God?

14

Stooping very low

Reading: John 13:1–17

It was just before the Passover Feast. Jesus knew that the time had come for him to leave this world and go to the Father. Having loved his own who were in the world, he now showed them the full extent of his love.

The evening meal was being served, and the devil had already prompted Judas Iscariot, son of Simon, to betray Jesus. Jesus knew that the Father had put all things under his power, and that he had come from God and was returning to God; so he got up from the meal, took off his outer clothing, and wrapped a towel round his waist. After that, he poured water into a basin and began to wash his disciples' feet, drying them with the towel that was wrapped around him.

He came to Simon Peter, who said to him, 'Lord, are you going to wash my feet?'

Jesus replied, 'You do not realise now what I am doing, but later you will understand.'

'No,' said Peter, 'you shall never wash my feet.'

Jesus answered, 'Unless I wash you, you have no part with me.'

'Then, Lord,' Simon Peter replied, 'not just my feet but my hands and my head as well!'

Jesus answered, 'A person who has had a bath needs only to wash his feet; his whole body is clean. And you are clean, though not every one of you.' For he knew

*who was going to betray him, and that was why he said
not every one was clean.*

   *When he had finished washing their feet, he put on his
clothes and returned to his place. 'Do you understand
what I have done for you?' he asked them. 'You call
me "Teacher" and "Lord", and rightly so, for that is
what I am. Now that I, your Lord and Teacher, have
washed your feet, you also should wash one another's
feet. I have set you an example that you should do as
I have done for you. I tell you the truth, no servant is
greater than his master, nor is a messenger greater than
the one who sent him. Now that you know these things,
you will be blessed if you do them.'*

If there is one word to sum up the ministry of Jesus, it
is this: service. His whole ministry was one of service.
This is apparent from the general tenor of the Gospel
narrative, and from many specific utterances. 'The Son
of Man came not to be served but to serve, and to give
his life as a ransom for many,' he told his followers. As he
took the way to the cross, he made it clear that service was
to be the hallmark of all Christian ministry. In contrast to
worldly rulers, preoccupied with status and authority, 'It
shall not,' he said, 'be so among you; but whoever would
be great among you must be your servant, and whoever
would be first among you must be slave of all.'

   This lesson of the royalty of service must have been
imprinted indelibly on the minds of the disciples by what
happened at the Last Supper. In the Middle East feet
quickly get hot and dusty, and it was the job of the
household slave to wash them. At the Last Supper there
was no household slave.

None of the apostles was willing to lose face by doing the slave's job; so they sat with unwashed feet. We can imagine the amazement when Jesus rose from supper and laid aside his garments. Wrapping a towel round his waist, he began to wash their feet. He was introducing them to a revolutionary idea of greatness – measured in terms of service. Relentlessly he pressed the point home.

There is, I think, a hint in St Luke's account that this action of Jesus arose out of a quarrel among the disciples over precedence and status. Although he does not record the foot washing, Luke does tell us of this devastating question which Jesus asked them at the meal: 'For which is the greater, one who sits at table or one who serves? Is it not the one who sits at table? But I am among you as one who serves.' Once more Jesus makes it crystal clear that what is true of him must be true of his disciples. 'The kings of the Gentiles exercise lordship over them . . . but not so with you; rather let the greatest among you become as the youngest, and the leader as one who serves.'

The Christian Church has found this a very hard lesson to swallow. Almost all consideration of church unity revolves round discussions on the validity of orders, their regularity, their authentication and their apostolicity. That is very natural. It is the way of the world. But it is not the way of Jesus Christ. He saw ministry not in terms of status but in terms of function. The pattern he set was the pattern of service. Of course, the very word 'ministry' means 'service'. But for Jesus this was no idle euphemism. It is no accident that the term 'ministry' is used to describe the whole of his public life and work. He was supremely and in everything the Servant of the Lord. That was his glory. He looked for no other. And so it must be with any ministry which claims to be truly Christian.

Reflection

Look back slowly over this week: when have you 'lorded
it over' people, and when have you lived as 'one who
serves?' Be honest but not over-critical, and come to God
in penitence for the times you have been overbearing and
ask him to help you live a life that reflects the ministry of
Jesus more closely.

Imagine the scene at the Last Supper, as Jesus washed
the feet of his disciples. What if Jesus came to you now,
picked up your tired, dirty, smelly feet in his hands and
washed them? How would it make you feel? Would you
try to stop him? Why? How might you feel afterwards?
Take note of your feelings, and bring them before God
in prayer.

For further study
How does the pattern of ministry in your church reflect
the ministry of service exemplified by Jesus? In what ways
does it *not* reflect it?

15

Hoping for heaven

Reading: Luke 12:16–21

And Jesus told them this parable: 'The ground of a certain rich man produced a good crop. He thought to himself, "What shall I do? I have no place to store my crops."

'Then he said, "This is what I'll do. I will tear down my barns and build bigger ones, and there I will store all my grain and my goods. And I'll say to myself, 'You have plenty of good things laid up for many years. Take life easy; eat, drink and be merry.'"

'But God said to him, "You fool! This very night your life will be demanded from you. Then who will get what you have prepared for yourself?"

'This is how it will be with anyone who stores up things for himself but is not rich towards God.'

The New Testament writers make a point of telling us that we are not put right with God by anything that we do; rather by something done for us. The worldly one's religion has two letters in it: 'do'. The forgiven sinner's has four: 'done'. And in that 'done' countless people of every age and culture have found peace. 'There is no condemnation to the one who is in Christ Jesus,' writes Paul. 'For what our attempts to keep the law could never do God himself has done through the person and the death of Jesus.' Done! It reminds me of the little girl who was so thrilled when she came to understand the meaning of the cross. 'I'm trusting in the justice of God, Mummy,' she cried. 'You mean in the love of God, dear?' corrected her mother. 'Oh no,' said the little girl. 'Jesus has died and paid all my debts. And God won't charge me for them again. I'm trusting in the justice of God.' How right she was.

I met this summer a remarkable man, quiet, confident. He had been a dance-band leader. And on his way home in the car one night he had been listening to a snatch of a religious radio programme. The preacher asked, 'If you were to die tonight, what possible reason is there why God should allow you into his heaven?' That seemed to James Kennedy a good question. So he did not rest until he discovered the answer. He knew that if his acceptance depended on his own good deeds he would have every reason to feel despondent. But he came to see that it didn't depend on anything of the sort. His acceptance, his pardon, his future with God depended simply and solely on what God had done to make him acceptable: it rested on the cross of Jesus Christ. That discovery revolutionised his life. He trained for ordination and is now exercising a remarkable ministry in the USA in which this question, that changed his life, features largely. Hundreds if not thousands of people each year come to God through the outreach of that church, as its members go round visiting and asking folk, 'If you died tonight, what good reason is there why God should accept you into his heaven?'

What would you say to that question? If you are just a churchgoer, if you are an 'I do my best' type, you would be bound to hesitate before answering. You would be suitably modest and non-committal. But the believer can say with joy and confidence, 'I know I would be accepted if I died tonight. Indeed, I am accepted now, and I have many promises of the New Testament to assure me of it. You see, I am trusting not in anything that I do for acceptance with God, but on what he has done. That is why I can be sure about it. My future is guaranteed by Calvary.'

Reflection

In your heart of hearts, how confident are you of your future with God? How do you feel about it? Grateful? Afraid? Unsure? Bring your feelings to God either in worship and wonder or in honest expression of your uncertainty. If it's the latter, then ask him to give you some assurance.

In what ways does your concept of future acceptance by God affect your attitude to the things that make up your daily life? Think especially of aspects such as dying and death, bereavement, personal danger, material possessions.

16

Making all things new

Reading: Matthew 9:18–34

While he was saying this, a ruler came and knelt before him and said, 'My daughter has just died. But come and put your hand on her, and she will live.' Jesus got up and went with him, and so did his disciples.

Just then a woman who had been subject to bleeding for twelve years came up behind him and touched the edge of his cloak. She said to herself, 'If I only touch his cloak, I will be healed.'

Jesus turned and saw her. 'Take heart, daughter,' he said, 'your faith has healed you.' And the woman was healed from that moment.

When Jesus entered the ruler's house and saw the flute players and the noisy crowd, he said, 'Go away. The girl is not dead but asleep.' But they laughed at him. After the crowd had been put outside, he went in and took the girl by the hand, and she got up. News of this spread through all that region.

As Jesus went on from there, two blind men followed him, calling out, 'Have mercy on us, Son of David!'

When he had gone indoors, the blind men came to him, and he asked them, 'Do you believe that I am able to do this?'

'Yes, Lord,' they replied.

Then he touched their eyes and said, 'According to your faith will it be done to you;' and their sight was restored. Jesus warned them sternly, 'See that no one knows about this.' But they went out and spread the news about him all over that region.

While they were going out, a man who was demon-possessed and could not talk was brought to Jesus. And when the demon was driven out, the man who had been dumb spoke. The crowd was amazed and said, 'Nothing like this has ever been seen in Israel.'

But the Pharisees said, 'It is by the prince of demons that he drives out demons.'

Newness is perhaps the dominant theme in this trio of miracles. First we find the double healing of two women, then the healing of two blind men and finally the healing of a dumb man. All of these are *amme-ha'aaretz*, 'people of the land'. They are the unprivileged, the outcasts. A woman with a menstrual flow was unclean. So was a dead girl. And the blind and dumb were outsiders. And by definition, an *am-ha'aretz* could not be holy. The rabbis were clear about that. Jesus scorns public opinion. A rabbi would never bother with the *amme-ha'aaretz*, but Jesus cares for the despised outsider. New sight for the blind, new speech for the dumb, new health for the sick, new life for the dead. That is what the newness of Jesus means! And that is what these three miracles are intended to teach. What marvellous preaching material they make. How apt to the continuing mission of the Church in Matthew's day, struggling against the syncretism of the pagan world.

There are several points which these three stories stress in common. Yes, the new has come, but it is only accessible to faith. That is the clear burden of all

three of these miracles. In each one, faith is the hand that
grasps the astonishing new thing presented in Jesus. Faith
is what brings us into contact with Jesus. It was so with the
woman in the crowd, and with the little girl: both touched,
and so experienced, his power. It was the same, too, with
the demonised man who could not speak. It was when he
was brought face to face with Jesus that he was set free.
Faith is not an intellectual construct: it is a primary form
of cognition, like touch.

Even if it is full of error and inadequacy, faith can avail,
so long as it is located in Jesus. As a matter of fact, the
evangelist draws attention to the very imperfect faith of
all three people in these stories. The synagogue ruler came
to Jesus as a last resort, desperate to see if anything could
be done about his child. The woman in the crowd had a
very superstitious faith: she thought that if she touched
his clothes the miracle might occur. The blind men called
Jesus 'Son of David', a title which, though true, was one
he sought to avoid because of its nationalistic associations.
Defective faith all round, but it availed, because it reached
out and touched Jesus. Faith brings salvation, and it does
so as soon as you stretch out and make contact with the
Lord. That is the message. 'Your faith has saved you.'
'Do you believe that I am able . . .?' That is the critical
question to the two blind men. When they replied 'Yes,
Lord' they received what they had asked for. The ruler of
the synagogue got more than he dreamed possible.

However, the power of Jesus is not displayed in the
climate of unbelief. The crowd round the woman did
not believe, and they received nothing. The professional
mourners round the girl did not believe, and they were
ejected. The Pharisees did not believe and like the crowd
they despised, they too received nothing. It is possible
to jostle Jesus in the crowd and still remain utterly
unchanged. It is possible to see miracle after miracle and
ascribe them to the devil's activity. It is not the case, as
people sometimes say that 'If only I'd been there I would
have believed.' No, there were plenty of people there

who did not believe although unimpeachable evidence was spread repeatedly before their eyes. The human heart is capable of profound resistance and deep self-deception. It is only when you trust that you find salvation. The faith may be a last resort, it may be superstitious, it may be theologically deficient. But if it is placed in Jesus, it binds the sinner and the Saviour together. And that is what he came to bring about.

Reflection

What examples, in your own life or that of others, have you seen of Jesus making things *new* – perhaps in the form of new life, or new hope, new love, or new circumstances – in response to faith, however weak or defective?

'Faith is not an intellectual construct: it is a primary form of cognition, like touch.' Most of the time we don't think about our senses: we just use them. When one is damaged, or lost, we flounder. Look back over the last twenty-four hours: can you think of ways in which you have 'just used' your faith? When your faith is weak or failing, how does it affect your daily life?

Take some time to thank God for the faith that you have, and ask him to strengthen it and to make it truly intrinsic to your very existence.

For further study
How might you counter the Pharisees' opinion that the miracles of Jesus were actually the work of the devil?

17

Copying the Master

Reading: John 15:9–17

As the Father has loved me, so have I loved you. Now remain in my love. If you obey my commands, you will remain in my love, just as I have obeyed my Father's commands and remain in his love. I have told you this so that my joy may be in you and that your joy may be complete. My command is this: Love each other as I have loved you. Greater love has no-one than this, that one lay down his life for his friends. You are my friends if you do what I command. I no longer call you servants, because a servant does not know his master's business. Instead, I have called you friends, for everything that I learned from my Father I have made known to you. You did not choose me, but I chose you to go and bear fruit – fruit that will last. Then the Father will give you whatever you ask in my name. This is my command: Love each other.

The first Christians spoke of Jesus *risen*. The major emphasis of their preaching was on the one who broke the power of death and rose on the first Easter Day. 'We are all witnesses,' they insisted. This confident assertion both of the resurrection of Jesus and of their relationship with him runs throughout the Acts. It comes in every evangelistic address recorded in the book. It is a major theme. I wonder if our contemporaries would say the same about our preaching? Are we always indicating that Jesus is not dead but alive, and that we know him? The churches which are growing these days are churches like that.

I recall a few years ago seeing written all over the walls of Oxford, 'Ché lives'. He didn't, of course. Ché Guevara, the self-sacrificing leader, was dead, even though his fame and ideology lived on in Bolivia and more widely in Latin America. The Messianic myth, for such it was, proved fragile at its most crucial point. The man was dead, and he did not rise. But since then many thousands of people have turned to Christ in Bolivia where Ché used to operate. And on the walls of Oxford you can often see scrawled a different legend: 'Jesus lives'.

They spoke of Jesus *reigning*. The one who had embodied God's sacrificial love now shared the throne of God. They were persuaded of it. There is nothing more regal in the whole universe than the self-sacrificial love of God. We have spurned it, but it will not let us go. That is the principle which people at their best most admire – in the mother or father sacrificing themselves for their children, or the captain for the ship. And that is the principle which God rates most highly. I think it is important for us in evangelism to help people escape from their childhood image of 'gentle Jesus meek and mild' and realise that in him they are confronting the very essence of the universe, a God who gives and gives, whatever our response – or lack of it. He is enthroned on high, and he awaits our loyal allegiance. The only indestructible thing in the whole cosmos is this self-abandoning love. Unless we are touched by it, respond to it, and begin to model it, we are ultimately on the road to destruction.

They spoke of a *contemporary* Jesus. He is no mere figure of long ago, but our contemporary. That is how they understood the Holy Spirit who was so manifestly among them. He is the presence of Jesus for today, released from the limitations of a physical body. The early Christians seem to have recognised from the outset that their experience of the Spirit was a continuation of their experience of Jesus. The Spirit was the means by which their Master kept them company. No longer was he the fitful, subpersonal manifestation of the naked might of God, as so often in Old Testament days. He was God's mighty presence, brought to them in Jesus. 'The Spirit,' they maintained, 'has come and changed our lives. He can do it for you.' Had all Christian evangelists given this stress on the person and work of the third person of the Trinity, there would have been less talk of the 'baptism of the Holy Spirit' as a second initiatory experience, and less confusion over his gifts and graces.

Reflection

'The only indestructible thing in the whole cosmos is this self-abandoning love. Unless we are touched by it, respond to it, and begin to model it, we are ultimately on the road to destruction.' In what ways have you been touched by this love of God? How have you responded? Try to remember specific instances and write them down. How did you feel on these occasions? How do you feel now, when you consider the love of God for you?

Who are the people who have modelled the love of God to you? In what ways have they modelled it? How might you model this love to others today?

Put your response to God's love into words and compose a prayer of love and allegiance to him.

18

Breaking down the barriers

Reading: Hebrews 10:19–24

Therefore, brothers, since we have confidence to enter the Most Holy Place by the blood of Jesus, by a new and living way opened for us through the curtain, that is, his body, and since we have a great priest over the house of God, let us draw near to God with a sincere heart in full assurance of faith, having our hearts sprinkled to cleanse us from a guilty conscience and having our bodies washed with pure water. Let us hold unswervingly to the hope we profess, for he who promised is faithful. And let us consider how we may spur one another on towards love and good deeds

The New Testament writers assert by a variety of images that Jesus, through his death and resurrection, has blazed a trail into the very presence of God for us to follow. And this is an important and relevant aspect of the atonement which is much neglected by contemporary preachers. People today feel lonely and cut off. They frequently feel shut off from the places of decision-making and power.

'There is no way out, or round, or through,' concluded H. G. Wells in his last book, *Mind at the End of its Tether*. In every trade dispute people are looking for a 'breakthrough'. In the Theatre of the Absurd a major theme was 'No Exit'. And that is how a great many people feel. They cannot get through.

The most startling teaching on this subject comes in Mark's account of the passion. The climax of his story is in 15:37, as Jesus dies. Then he takes us away from Golgotha back to the city and informs us that the curtain of the temple was ripped in half from top to bottom. Then immediately back to the site of execution, and the centurion's confession 'Truly this man was the Son of God.' And all in three verses! Is this literary incompetence? Or had Mark a deep purpose?

The curtain in the temple was no ordinary one. It was sixty feet high, and very thick. It was designed to keep people out of the Holy of Holies, the place which God inhabited. That curtain spelt the message 'Keep out'.

So what is Mark trying to teach us? Surely, that the death of Jesus made a permanent way through to the presence of God. It blazed a trail through the barriers. The quarantine was ended. The 'No Entry' signs were removed. If one of us had split the curtain, it would have been from the bottom to the top. Mark tells us that it was rent from top to bottom: God's work, no less. And that spells access. There is a way through.

Mark's artistry is not done. He moves to the man in charge of Jesus' execution, and records a strange comment he made. 'Truly this man was the Son of God.' On Roman lips this would express admiration of Jesus as a superb man. But of course Mark means us to see more in the comment than that. It is as if the first Gentile is availing himself of the access provided within the curtain, into God's very presence. For the Christian baptismal confession was precisely this: 'Jesus Christ, Son of God, Saviour.' In that centurion we are meant to see the first Gentile entering into the Holy of Holies, saved by the death of a Jew. The first access into the presence of God is offered to the man who had slain his Son! Abundant access, indeed.

But that is what God is like. That is the astonishing love he shows to those who reject him. That is grace indeed.

And Hebrews 10:19 picks up this incident and meditates on it. It sees the curtain, keeping us out. And then, as in a twin projector, one picture fades into another. That curtain is replaced by Jesus Christ on the cross. His wounds replace the split in the curtain. This is a new thing in the history of the world. The blood sacrifice had to be offered afresh each year when the high priest had gone in. But the blood of Jesus is described as 'ever fresh', its validity eternal. The high priest of Israel went in with the names of the tribes of Israel on his garments, although they could never follow him. This high priest had blazed a trail within that curtain which his disciples were entitled to follow. They could enter behind their high priest, for the curtain had been torn asunder and the blood was ever fresh.

The implications of this for people today are immensely suggestive. It is not true that there is no exit. It is not true that there is no way out or round or through. It is not true that we are imprisoned within inexorable circumstances, or that breakthrough is impossible. Jesus has broken through! I need not remain shut in and cut off. The heavens are not brass, nor the universe silent. In Christ my trail-blazer I can get through. And is not that precisely what people today need to hear?

Reflection

'Let us draw near to God with a sincere heart in full assurance of faith, having our hearts sprinkled to cleanse us from a guilty conscience and having our bodies washed with pure water.' How do you feel about drawing near to God? Are there barriers of your own that need to be broken down? What are they? Try to visualise the deep cleansing that this verse describes: what are the areas of your life that most need it? Do you *want* to be washed clean, or do you cling to ways of living which you suspect are not what God wants for you, but of which you feel unable to let go? Be honest and open before God. He wants you to draw near to him: what do *you* want?

What barriers can you identify between today's society and God? Where have they come from? How do they prevent people from coming close to God?

For further study
What contemporary images can you think of for the breaking of barriers? How can they help you to understand what Jesus has done?

19

Conquering everything

Reading: Revelation 5:5, 9–12

One of the elders said to me, 'Do not weep! See, the Lion of the tribe of Judah, the Root of David, has triumphed. He is able to open the scroll and its seven seals.'
And they sang a new song:

'You are worthy to take the scroll
and to open the seals,
because you were slain,
and with your blood you purchased men for God
from every tribe and language and people and nation.
You have made them to be a kingdom
and priests to serve our God,
and they will reign on the earth.'

Then I looked and heard the voice of many angels, numbering thousands upon thousands, and ten thousand times ten thousand. They encircled the throne and the living creatures and the elders. In a loud voice they sang:

'Worthy is the Lamb, who was slain,
to receive power and wealth and wisdom and strength
and honour and glory and praise!'

The supreme paradox of Calvary is this: it looks like defeat, but is a victory. The throne of the universe belongs to self-sacrificial love. The cross is the supreme glory of the Servant Messiah. There is no lifting up higher than the gibbet of Calvary. It is there that we see the glory and the exaltation of the Saviour.

The account of the passion is full of profound irony. As Jesus is put on trial for his life, who is the real victor? A terrified governor? Roman justice? A squad of soldiers? Religious intransigence? No. Jesus is clearly portrayed as the victor. Pilate could have no power over him had not God given it to him. It is God and God's Servant who hold ultimate power. Power is only delegated temporarily to earthly rulers. Jesus is portrayed as the victor. He even 'dismisses' his spirit. Christ is the conqueror on that dark day. The victim is in charge of events.

This aspect of the passion receives much attention in the New Testament, and nowhere more than in the Book of Revelation, which concentrates the reader's gaze on the throne of God. The Lord is reigning. The Lamb with the marks of slaughter on him is in the midst of the throne. No wonder the redeemed break out 'worthy are thou . . .' For there is no power in the universe greater than self-sacrificing love. Nothing can obliterate it. Nothing has obliterated it.

Jesus is conqueror over suffering. He shared our pains. He drained the cup of suffering to the dregs. And he rose again. He will finally wipe away every tear from every eye. 'Neither shall there be mourning nor crying nor pain any more, for the former things have passed away.'

Jesus is conqueror over opposition. Nobody enjoys it, least of all from friends. Jesus showed us how to take it without bitterness or retaliation. The Lion of Judah turned out to be the Lamb. He was the non-violent conqueror over violent opposition and flagrant injustices. And he lives, and is with his beleaguered servants as they face the hatred and cruelty of a hard world.

Jesus is conqueror over the world. To each of the

Seven Churches he, the conqueror, promises to recognise those who in his strength overcome the world. The pressures deriving from social conformity, political persuasion, economic boycott, financial stringency, and the general climate of a society which leaves God out of account can be overcome. Jesus did it. And he lives on in his followers.

Jesus is conqueror over evil. He faced every combination of wickedness on the cross, and he overcame. He achieved the defeat of every evil power ranged against him by absorbing their venom into himself – and rising triumphant. The cross spelt the defeat of evil in God's world. That tree was for the healing of the nation.

Jesus is conqueror over the devil. It is a shallow theology which dismisses Satan as unreal. The great anti-God force is very much in business still. But he is still a defeated foe. He met his match in Christ on Calvary. That victory presaged the final banishment of Satan to the bottomless pit. And it meant that, though hard beset, the followers of Jesus can join the host of heaven, and exult 'Now the salvation and the kingdom of our God and the authority of his Christ have come, for the accuser of our brethren has been thrown down, who accuses them day and night before our God. And they have conquered him by the blood of the Lamb, and by the word of their testimony, for they loved not their lives even unto death.'

Jesus is conqueror over death itself. 'Fear not,' he says to us, 'I am the first and the last, and the living one. I died, and behold I am alive for evermore, and I hold the keys of death and hades.' That resurrection of his on the first Easter Day is the guarantee that 'death shall be no more'.

What a conqueror! In his company we can face any problem, any circumstance, with joyful anticipation. Christians should be totally distinctive in this respect. 'In the world you shall have tribulation,' he had told them. 'But be of good cheer. I have overcome the world.' If the Church is to regain its credibility in society, its members must be helped to see that they have all power in heaven and earth available to them in Jesus Christ their Lord. They must celebrate his victory in every circumstance of life and death. That is both a challenge and a possibility for the disciples of Jesus the conqueror.

Reflection

'In his company we can face any problem, any circumstance, with joyful anticipation.' Consider some of the problems you have faced in the past, or may be facing now. What difference has the company of Christ made to you? The knowledge that Christ is there with us can give enormous strength, but sometimes it is difficult to *feel* his presence. How can you apply this knowledge, and take strength from it when you don't feel anything? You may find it helpful to talk to others about this and learn from their experiences.

In what ways do you come up against suffering, opposition, worldliness, evil or death? What strength can you draw from the supreme victory of Christ as you face these forces?

We sometimes get so overwhelmed by the difficulties we find ourselves in, or that we observe others in, that we forget that Christ is conqueror of all. Think of some particular situations and use your imagination to bring the conquering Christ into them. What difference could he make? How does this exercise affect your attitude to the difficulties?

20

Dismantling the divisions

Reading: Matthew 5:13–16

*'You are the salt of the earth. But if the salt loses its
saltiness, how can it be made salty again? It is no longer
good for anything, except to be thrown out and trampled
by men.*

*'You are the light of the world. A city on a hill cannot
be hidden. Neither do people light a lamp and put it
under a bowl. Instead they put it on its stand, and it
gives light to everyone in the house. In the same way,
let your light shine before men, that they may see your
good deeds and praise your Father in heaven.'*

Jesus was a secular person. He did not keep himself
in splendid separation from the defilements of secular
society. He knew where the prostitutes and the soldiers,
the tax-gatherers and the poorest of the poor were to be
found. And he got among them. He completely fulfilled
the ideal he taught of being 'in the world, yet not of
the world'. People did not feel that he was talking down
to them or manifesting superiority. They were drawn

by his naturalness, his integrity, his unshockability, his friendliness, his holiness. For true holiness is the greatest magnet of all. And we? We tend to keep our evangelism for church, if we do it at all. We talk of God in church, but rarely outside. We move in church circles, and simply do not know where or how to get among the vast numbers of utterly unchurched people around us. Our churches have many programmes for members, but little that the man in the street can identify with. An invisible wall separates the church from society. We are not, in the best sense of the word, secular people. Yet if the incarnation means anything to us, it should have spelled the collapse of any dividing wall between the secular and the sacred.

Jesus was a caring person. It was not all talk and no action. Preaching and acts of compassion and power went hand in hand in his ministry. He healed broken people. He liberated demonised people. He met lonely people. On occasion, he raised dead people back to life again. Practical caring is not always associated with Christian evangelism. We are perceived to be people who have something to say, maybe, but who do not do anything.

The professor of evangelism at Fuller Seminary, Bill Pannell, stresses the need not only for a Billy Graham but for a Martin Luther King in evangelism. The latter would not see the garbage heaps in Manila as merely a pressing incentive to preach the gospel:

He could tell us about garbage and garbage workers. He could make the connection between the dump and politics. He could show us the connections between poverty in Manila and racism in Washington D.C. He could remind us that there is a difference between righteousness and relief, between preaching and martyrdom. He could demonstrate that you can see the promised land from a garbage heap much better than from a cathedral, or a well furnished hotel down-town. Christians who act in solidarity with the denizens of garbage dumps get themselves shot. Hardly anyone shoots evangelists

*any more, as long as they stick to the simple gospel,
anyway.*

Jesus was a community person. The community of the
three close followers, the community of the twelve, of the
seventy . . . You find him in homes as diverse as those of
Lazarus, Martha and Mary on the one hand, and Jairus on
the other – with Zacchaeus and Simon the Pharisee thrown
in for good measure. You find him with the crowds. You
find him founding a new community, bound together by a
new covenant. He was the very antithesis of individualism.
And yet, supreme irony, his Western followers are shame-
less individualists. So individualist that many of us treat
church as an optional extra. So individualist that meeting
in a home for Christian fellowship of an informal nature,
or even greeting one another with a handshake or embrace
in church, are seen as a threat. So individualist that we sit
as far apart from one another as we can when we gather
for worship. And on top of it all, we are split up into
endless – and proliferating – denominations. And yet we
are the people whom God has chosen to show to the world
a foretaste of heaven, a pattern of his new society!

Is not this almost total lack of Christian solidarity why
trade unions have largely separated themselves from
their Christian roots? Is this not why Marxism is more
appealing to the poor of the world than Christianity?
Is this solidarity not what binds Muslims together into
such a formidable force while Christians have so little
to show in terms of fellowship and unity? Evangelism
will not be effective unless it springs from community,
and draws people into community: a community which
is warm, accepting, unjudging and supportive. That will
touch people at a level reason alone cannot reach.

And finally, Jesus was a passionately committed person.
He came proclaiming and embodying the kingdom of God.
All he did, all he said, was directed towards extending its
boundaries. There was nothing impatient about his man-
ner, nothing brash about his insistence, nothing insensitive

about his relationships. But it was impossible to mistake
the purpose of his life, and the joy and conviction he had
in sharing it. That is not the impression which generally
emerges from contemporary Christian circles. But when
it is present, it speaks. It is so real, so authentic, that it cuts
through arguments and excuses. It is very attractive. In a
grey world, people long for sunshine; and when they see
it shining brightly and unashamedly in another person's
life, they are drawn to enquire about it. Evangelism then
becomes easy.

Reflection

Take a look at how you have spent your time over the
last few days or weeks. What are your priorities, and
how do you decide them? Write them down now, and
look prayerfully at what you have written. Can you
distinguish between 'sacred' and 'secular' activities? Ask
God if there is anything he would like you to change:
ask if he gives things the same importance that you do.
If Jesus were living your life, would he spend your time
in the same way?

Focus on the image of light from the Bible passage and pray about your involvement in the world around you. Light shines: the only way to avoid it is to keep your eyes closed – unless it is kept hidden, in which case it may as well not be there at all. Ask God to show you how you can let your light shine, and how you can work towards the collapse of any dividing wall that exists between the secular and the sacred.

For further study
'We are perceived to be people who have something to say, maybe, but who do not do anything.' In your experience, how valid is this judgment? What does your church have to offer the person in the street?

21

Changing direction

Reading: Luke 19:1–10

Jesus entered Jericho and was passing through. A man was there by the name of Zacchaeus; he was a chief tax collector and was wealthy. He wanted to see who Jesus was, but being a short man he could not, because of the crowd. So he ran ahead and climbed a sycamore-fig tree to see him, since Jesus was coming that way.

When Jesus reached the spot, he looked up and said to him, 'Zacchaeus, come down immediately. I must stay at your house today.' So he came down at once and welcomed him gladly.

All the people saw this and began to mutter, 'He has gone to be the guest of a "sinner."'

But Zacchaeus stood up and said to the Lord, 'Look, Lord! Here and now I give half of my possessions to the poor, and if I have cheated anybody out of anything, I will pay back four times the amount.'

Jesus said to him, 'Today salvation has come to this house, because this man, too, is a son of Abraham. For the Son of Man came to seek and to save what was lost.'

It was a hot afternoon, and I was watching him chat to the large number of elderly people who had gathered for their regular informal Thursday afternoon meeting. I was struck by the way he seemed to care. Then I met his wife, and I noticed their relaxed trust in one another and their obvious harmony. I remarked to my friend the vicar that he had got a splendid new assistant, even if he was a bit older than most. Then he told me the story. Actually, I could not do better than give it to you in the assistant's own words:

When I was in my early thirties, I became involved with another woman. I fell deep into sin – sin of the ugliest kind – which made me reject all thoughts of God and which very nearly broke up our family life. Five months in a neurosis hospital under the care of some of the finest psychiatrists made no difference to my attitude to life. I came out of hospital worse than when I went in. I had developed a terrible stammer; I took drugs at night to try to help me sleep; I took pep pills during the day to try to keep me going; I went out of my way to avoid contact with anyone at all; I fainted in the streets and I jeered at anyone who tried to help me. I was determined to carry on with my selfish and sinful way of life, no matter what hurt it caused other people.

Then one Christmas, my son Alan (who was then just eight years old) gave me a picture of the Lord Jesus standing at the door, knocking. 'Behold, I stand at the door and knock; if any one hears my voice and opens the door, I will come in to him and eat with him, and he with me.' For a long time I deliberately turned away from that picture. But the knocking became more and more insistent until finally, at 10.00 p.m. on the 26th June, 1961, in utter desperation and almost unbelief, I said, 'Lord, you say you can change people's lives – come into my heart and change mine.' At last I had taken that step of faith, and immediately my prayer was answered. There was a complete transformation in my life from that moment onwards.

Undoubtedly there was. It was perfectly obvious, even to the casual observer. Once devoted to self, he was now an ordained minister, giving himself for others. Once ruining his family life by another woman, he was now happily reunited with his wife, and at one with her in the work of the Lord. Once dependent on drugs for excitement, he was now alive with Christ's joy and love. Quite a change. And nowhere greater than in his relationships with others. It doesn't take much imagination to think what a different place his home is, now . . .

And home is the place to begin. Jesus once healed a man who had serious psychological trouble. The man wanted to accompany him as a disciple on a roving ministry. In a way that would have been much easier for him. But Jesus said: 'No. Go back home to your folks, and let them know what wonderful things the Lord has done for you.' Christianity, like charity, begins at home.

Reflection

In what ways has God changed your heart in the past? In what ways do you think it still needs to be changed? If you can't think of anything, ask God to show you.

How does your allegiance to Jesus show itself in your daily life, particularly at home? How would you most like it to be recognised?

22

Substituting goodness

Reading: Romans 5:6–11

You see, at just the right time, when we were still powerless, Christ died for the ungodly. Very rarely will anyone die for a righteous man, though for a good man someone might possibly dare to die. But God demonstrates his own love for us in this: While we were still sinners, Christ died for us.

Since we have now been justified by his blood, how much more shall we be saved from God's wrath through him! For if, when we were God's enemies, we were reconciled to him through the death of his Son, how much more, having been reconciled, shall we be saved through his life! Not only is this so, but we also rejoice in God through our Lord Jesus Christ, through whom we have now received reconciliation.

Why was the death of Jesus so important? Basically because ours is a broken and sinful world. And sin matters to God. He cannot overlook it. His wrath, that is to say his personal though not vindictive reaction against sin, is active. In the end, it is a blessing that this is so. It would be no comfort to us if God pretended that evil did not matter. For then good would not matter either. God would not be a loving Creator but an indifferent fiend. God's holiness and our sin can no more mix than can light and dark, oil and water. Separation between the parties is inevitable. If it is not dealt with, this separation will be final. And physical death will put the final seal on that separation. That, incidentally, is why people feel God to be so far away: our sins separate him from us. And that is what brought Jesus to Calvary. He came to share, and so to remove our alienation. He came to take our place as sinner though he was Son of God, in order that we, though sinners, might share his place as children of God.

But why was it necessary that Christ should die on a cross, that very unJewish means of execution? Here again the answer lies in the long shadow cast by the Old Testament. Deuteronomy 21:21f. makes it plain that anyone exposed to die upon a tree was to be seen as resting under the curse of God. It is, then, of the utmost significance that the New Testament writers do not shrink from repeatedly calling the cross a 'tree'. Paul's usage is particularly bold and explicit. He has just said in Galatians 3:10 that all of us lie under the curse of God for having broken his law: and three verses later he explains with triumphant joy, 'Christ redeemed us from the curse of the law, having become a curse for us – for it is written "Cursed is everyone who hangs upon a tree."' It is impossible to express this idea of substitution more clearly. Christ bore for us the judgment of his holy Father against sinners. We broke the law of God. He took the place of the lawbreakers.

All through the Bible there had been trailers of this epic event. The Passover Lamb. The Sin Offering. The Suffering Servant. And on Calvary all this was fulfilled. 'Christ died for sins, once and for all, the righteous for the unrighteous, that he might bring us to God.'

Substitution is not the only side of the cross. It is not

even the main thrust of New Testament teaching about the cross. But it does speak to troubled consciences as nothing else does. It is a truth, as we have seen in earlier chapters, which is all too easy to abuse. Analogies from lawcourts or the punishment of third parties are particularly to be eschewed. But despite the dangers of misunderstanding and misinterpretation, this mode of understanding Calvary is quite essential. It enables us to see how God could be both just and the justifier to whoever believes in Jesus. Stripped of all its legal imagery, it makes one central point which lies at the heart of the atonement. He did for me on Calvary all that was necessary to put me in a right relationship with God. And that is something I could never, never have done without him. It goes further. It makes the even more fundamental point that, but for the cross of Christ, God would not be to me what he is. Calvary did not merely show something: the love of God. It achieved something: the reinstatement of sinners. And it cost the Son of God his life, no less.

There is nothing automatic about this reinstatement. We for our part need to stretch out our hand to the bloodstained hand of the Saviour. Only then is contact made. St Luke was clear about this in his account of the passion. One dying robber was saved on that terrible Good Friday, so that nobody need despair. But only one was saved, so that nobody could presume. And when people follow that penitent thief and entrust themselves to the Substitute, then like Bunyan's Pilgrim they can (and frequently do) give three jumps for joy as they see the burdens on their backs fall off and disappear into the bottomless pit opened up at the foot of Calvary's cross.

Reflection

How would you define 'sin'? Write it down. How much and what sort of influence do your feelings, your circumstances, or other people have on your attitude to sin?

'Our sins separate God from us.' We all sin, so the experience of feeling separated from God is common to each one of us. How do you recognise this separation when it happens? At this precise moment, do you feel God is close or far away? If you feel that he is far from you, and you know there are specific things you need his forgiveness for, then seek it now. But if you are not really sure why you feel such separation from him, ask God to show you. Either way, it is necessary for you to stretch out your hand to the bloodstained hand of the Saviour, in order to make contact with him. Jesus died so that you should not be alienated from God: you can therefore be utterly confident that, from his point of view, your continued closeness to him matters enormously.

For further study
The curse of the law is a Jewish concept that means little to most Westerners. So what can the belief that Jesus has redeemed you from it mean for *you*? Try to answer in concrete, tangible terms, and not in religious jargon!

23

Overcoming evil

Reading: Ephesians 6:10–17

Finally, be strong in the Lord and in his mighty power. Put on the full armour of God so that you can take your stand against the devil's schemes. For our struggle is not against flesh and blood, but against the rulers, against the authorities, against the powers of this dark world and against the spiritual forces of evil in the heavenly realms. Therefore put on the full armour of God, so that when the day of evil comes, you may be able to stand your ground, and after you have done everything, to stand. Stand firm then, with the belt of truth buckled around your waist, with the breastplate of righteousness in place, and with your feet fitted with the readiness that comes from the gospel of peace. In addition to all this, take up the shield of faith, with which you can extinguish all the flaming arrows of the evil one. Take the helmet of salvation and the sword of the Spirit, which is the word of God.

The triumph of Jesus Christ at every juncture over the powers and principalities of evil is a major theme of the New Testament. He was tested by persecution at his birth and throughout his life. He was tested by false friends, by hostile religious leaders, by Jewish and Gentile civil authorities. He was tested in the healings, the exorcisms, the temptations in the wilderness. The principalities and powers attacked him through opposition from within his own circle. His own family assigned his notoriety to the devil and one of his intimate friends sold him for thirty pieces of silver. No one was ever tested like Jesus Christ. He faced it all, and overcame it all, as no one before or since has done. The secret of his life was his determination to please his heavenly Father at all points. The spirits of disobedience had never before in the history of humanity discovered a person who was both totally obedient and totally fulfilled in that obedience. No wonder they could get no grip on him. The evil spirits perceived the ultimate judgment, and they realised that in Jesus Christ the end-time had broken in – and that his appearance in the world spelt their doom.

But it was at the cross that Jesus Christ won the greatest and most conclusive victory over the powers of evil. He destroyed their sovereignty by utterly submitting to it all the way to the scaffold. In submitting he conquered; just as, conversely, in rebelling they had fallen. Unlike Satan, unlike the powers, unlike Adam, Jesus had not considered being equal with God as a thing to be seized.

Behind the cross there lay, first and foremost, the design of the human heart. Basic human failings like pride, jealousy, and greed combined with the self-righteousness and traditionalism of Jewish religion, the injustice of Roman politics, and the apathy of the crowd to take Christ to that gibbet. But behind these religious, political and social pressures stood the principalities and powers of evil. Thus organised religion was there at the cross: all the more dangerous because masquerading as true religion. Politics were there at the cross: but behind Herod and Pilate, the earthly rulers, lay the invisible powers and it was they who crucified the Lord of glory. The average man and woman were there at the cross: but the New Testament takes us to a more profound level here too. When the crowd cried, 'His blood be upon us and upon our children', we see them driven by forces beyond themselves to a conclusion they could never have envisaged.

Second, behind the cross there lay the will of Jesus himself. He chose with his eyes open. He came to give his life as ransom for many. But here again we are driven to look deeper. Why was it necessary? Because of the grip the strong man had upon the house: the stronger than the strong was needed to set the place free. It was only by facing these forces in the place where they exercised their power that he could break that power. The cross was that place of victory over all the forces of the Enemy. By submitting in perfect obedience right up to death, he broke the power of him who held men and women in thralldom through its dread. In that cross he conquered.

Third, behind the cross there lay the predestination of God. If God ever acted in history he acted then. But look deeper. In that will of God we see not only his reconciliation of sinners but the complete rebuttal of dualism. These principalities and powers which thwart his will are not independent military units opposing his own army. They are rebel forces of his own. In Christ they were created and in Christ they were defeated. They must own his sway whether they like it or not. His lordship, since the resurrection, has been beyond cavil among beings celestial, terrestrial and subterranean. 'In the end,' writes James Stewart, 'the same invisible powers are the tribute which the Son hands over to the Father, that "God may be all in all".' He concludes that our real battle is not 'with Communism or Caesarism but with the invisible realm where sinister forces stand flaming and fanatic against the rule of Christ. And the only way to meet that demonic mystic passion is with the passion of the Lord.'

Reflection

In what ways are the powers of evil active in the world now? How do you come across them in your daily life? What is your role in countering them, and how can you fulfil that role?

'The spirits of disobedience had never before in the history of humanity discovered a person who was both totally obedient and totally fulfilled in that obedience.' What aspects of obedience do you struggle with? What help for yourself can you find in Jesus' fulfilment in obedience, and in his determination to please his Father at all points?

Bring your struggles before Christ now and pray that you may know his victory in them. Use the armour imagery from the Bible reading to pray for strength and protection against the powers of evil.

24

Practising perfection

Reading: 1 Peter 2:19–25

It is commendable if a man bears up under the pain of unjust suffering because he is conscious of God. But how is it to your credit if you receive a beating for doing wrong and endure it? But if you suffer for doing good and you endure it, this is commendable before God. To this you were called, because Christ suffered for you, leaving you an example, that you should follow in his steps.

> *'He committed no sin, and no deceit was found in his mouth.'*

When they hurled their insults at him, he did not retaliate; when he suffered, he made no threats. Instead, he entrusted himself to him who judges justly. He himself bore our sins in his body on the tree, so that we might die to sins and live for righteousness; by his wounds you have been healed. For you were like sheep going astray, but now you have returned to the Shepherd and Overseer of your souls.

Jesus' teaching, the highest ever given, was backed up by a flawless character. So flawless that when at his trial they put up false witnesses to arraign him they could not agree in their testimony. So flawless that Pilate three times declared him not guilty, and Pilate's wife had nightmares about the judicial murder of this innocent person. So flawless that the centurion at the cross, hardened as he was to bloodshed, declared: 'This man was innocent.'

So flawless that his friends – his friends, mark you – maintained that he was completely without sin. Indeed, tough fisherman though he was, Simon Peter once fell at his feet and begged him to depart from a soiled person like himself. So flawless that when faced by an angry crowd out for his blood, Jesus could calmly ask them: 'Which of you can point to anything wrong that I have done? – and get no reply. So flawless was his character that unlike the great saints of any religion, who are always the first to recognise their own shortcomings, Jesus could say, 'I always do what is pleasing to [my heavenly Father].'

Such was the man. Such was his conduct. There was no shadow of wickedness or failure in it. No other great teacher had ever managed to practise fully what he preached. Moses, Confucius, Plato – and in our own century Martin Luther King, Pope John Paul, and Billy Graham – have all taught wonderful things, and men have hung on their words. But none of them have managed to carry out what they taught. In all of them there has been some consciousness of failure and falling short of their own high ideals, let alone God's. But Jesus was different. He taught the highest standards that any teacher has ever formulated, and he kept them through and through. He utterly practised what he preached. His life was a moral miracle, and it has never been matched.

Perhaps that is why when he quietly claimed to be the supreme self-disclosure of God to humanity and the only way to enable people to know God as their Father, they believed him. He told them not to believe him if his 'works' did not match his 'words'. They did. He not only taught people to love their enemies: he did it. He not only claimed that the highest thing someone could do for their friends was to die for them: he did it. He not only taught that it was more blessed to give than to receive: he lived that way. It makes him the most remarkable of all teachers. Here was one who taught the most exacting standards and embodied them completely. He claimed to bring God into our midst; and his life lent credibility to his claim.

Reflection

What do you think it was about Jesus the man that drew people to him, even though his perfection would expose their lack of it? What was it that first drew *you* to Jesus, and what is it now that continues to do so? Try to express your feelings for Jesus in words or pictures, or sing a love song or hymn to him.

'Jesus utterly practised what he preached.' List some of the ways in which Jesus' life matched up so perfectly to his preaching. Be specific, and, as usual, don't resort to religious jargon. Now consider the way you yourself live your life, and ask God to show you ways in which you can follow Christ's example more closely.

For further study
Why was it necessary for Jesus' life and character to be flawless?

25

Seeking little children

Reading: Matthew 11:25–27

*At that time Jesus said, 'I praise you, Father, Lord of
heaven and earth, because you have hidden these things
from the wise and learned, and revealed them to little
children. Yes, Father, for this was your good pleasure.*

*'All things have been committed to me by my Father.
No one knows the Son except the Father, and no one
knows the Father except the Son and those to whom the
Son chooses to reveal him.'*

Jesus is quietly claiming to be the locus of all revelation.
Whatever revelation there may be, dispersed in human
intellect and values, in virtuous action, in nature, and
in the history of humanity, the centre of all God's self-
disclosure is Jesus of Nazareth. He is the fulfilment of
all the hopes of the Old Testament, and the heart of all
revelation. In a dark world lit by candles and lamps, he
comes as a searchlight.

If we look closely at this claim, we will see five distinct
elements in it.

First, Jesus maintains that God the Father conceals and reveals according to his will. People cannot grasp a Christian understanding of God and Christian relationship with God by their own efforts. They cannot discern who Jesus is, what the kingdom is, unless God shows them. He conceals these things from those who are wise in their own conceits, and reveals them to those who come with child-like trust and teachableness. Whenever anyone comes to faith, there is a divine disclosure to that person.

Second, Jesus claims to be the plenipotentiary representative of the Father. He comes from the Father's side, equipped with the Father's power and trenchancy, and displaying the compassion of the Father's heart. He fully represents God, and he comes with God's own claim on human hearts.

Third, only the Father fully understands Jesus. Not John, not the disciples, not 'the wise' or 'the babes'. The mystery of his person is inscrutable this side of heaven. Theologians have spent centuries seeking to reconcile his divine and human natures. It is like trying to square the circle. With the limited discernment of the human mind and heart it cannot be done. It takes God to know God. Only the Father knows the Son. What a claim!

Fourth, only Jesus fully understands the Father. Great men have discovered and taught many true and noble things about God. Nobody has known him with the intimacy of Jesus, who could call him '*Abba*', dear Daddy. When that holy man Mahatma Gandhi was dying, one of his relatives came to him and asked 'Babaki, you have been looking for God all your life. Have you found him yet?' 'No,' was the reply. 'I'm still looking.' The humility, the earnestness, the sheer goodness of a great teacher like Gandhi shine through a remark like that. But it stands in the most stark contrast with Jesus' claim in this passage. 'No man knows the Father except the Son.' He does not know something about God. He does not even know everything about God. He knows God absolutely. It is simply breath-taking.

And fifth, because Jesus shares the Father's nature as well as ours, he and he alone can reveal the Father. He can show us, because he knows. He can introduce us because he belongs: he is the Son.

These five elements go to make up the most astounding claim that has ever been heard on human lips, that the way to know the Father is through Jesus. It reminds us irresistibly of the words of Jesus in St John: 'I am the Way, the Truth and the Life. No one comes to the Father but by me' and 'He who has seen me has seen the Father.' If you want to know what God is like, look at Jesus. If you want to get through to God, come to Jesus. If you want to discover the epicentre of God's self-disclosure, you will find it in Jesus. That is the claim. That is what makes Christianity at once so widely attractive and so widely hated. The sheer exclusivity of the claims drive people in one direction or the other. They do not allow us the comfort of occupying middle ground. Nor can we shrug out of deciding by saying, 'Well, these exclusive claims are only in the fourth Gospel which may well be late and theologically tendentious.'

The passage before us is every bit as challenging, exclusive and absolute in its claim as anything in the fourth Gospel, and it is situated in one of the oldest strata of the Gospel tradition, the 'Q' material, sayings of Jesus found both in Matthew and Luke but absent from Mark. Scholars ascribe a very high degree of reliability to this material. C. S. Lewis is right. There is no way of reconciling Jesus' humility of lifestyle, quality of character and profundity of teaching with the rampant megalomania which must colour his theological claims about himself if he is not God. We are invited to choose how we shall respond to so staggering a claim.

Reflection

Spend a few moments contemplating the sheer wonder of Jesus, a man, so fully representing God. What does it tell you about Jesus? What does it tell you about God the Father? Write down your thoughts.

'People cannot discern who Jesus is, what the kingdom is, unless God shows them. He conceals these things from those who are wise in their own conceits, and reveals them to those who come with child-like trust and teachableness.' Think about your own experience of learning who Jesus is. What prompted your response to him? In what respects does 'child-like trust and teachableness' describe your faith? What can make it hard for you to trust in this way? Turn your thoughts into prayer by thanking God for all that you have learnt of him and asking for the grace to develop a faith that is truly child-like (not childish) and teachable.

For further study
'If you want to know what God is like, look at Jesus.' How could you back up this statement?

26

Giving rest to the weary

Reading: Matthew 11:28–30

*'Come to me, all you who are weary and burdened, and
I will give you rest. Take my yoke upon you and learn
from me, for I am gentle and humble in heart, and you
will find rest for your souls. For my yoke is easy and my
burden is light.'*

The revelation and the rescue belong together. So Jesus,
after making this claim to be the revelation of God, issues
the most wonderful, warm invitation to all who feel in
need of the rescue of God. Notice again the breath-taking
claim 'Come to me'. Not 'Go to God' – you could not find
the way. The Bible suggests that there is a twist in our
human nature which would make us unwilling to embrace
the highest when we see it. 'Come to me – I have come
to seek you out.' What grace! That God should come to
seek his rebel subjects with no word of condemnation on
his lips, but an invitation, 'Come'. That one word shows
us the very heart of God. That is his attitude to sinners.
The weary and the heavily burdened are particularly

invited. That may have a significance beyond the obvious,
for the Greeks were exhausted by the search for truth
which had been proceeding for centuries without resolu-
tion. They anticipated modern existentialists in concluding
that authentic experience was incommunicable: 'It is very
difficult to find God, and when you have found him it
is impossible to tell anyone else about him.' As for the
Jews, they must have found religion a great burden. It
had become a matter of endless regulations and duties.
Did not the scribes and Pharisees 'bind heavy burdens,
hard to bear, and lay them on men's shoulders'? Jesus
came to end the search by taking us in his loving arms.
He came to lift burdens off our aching backs, not tie them
on. He offers 'rest', not in the sense of cessation from toil,
but peace and fulfilment and a sense of being put right.
We have only to come, to entrust ourselves to him, and
we shall find that rest. Millions have done so, and have
enjoyed that given rest.

There is a deeper rest, which cannot be given but can
only be found, the rest of taking his yoke upon us and
entering into partnership with him. He wants not only to
welcome back the sinner, but to train the disciple. 'Come
to me' is followed by 'Take my yoke upon you'. The yoke
was the wooden collar that ran across the shoulders of a
pair of oxen and enabled them jointly to pull enormous
weights. Metaphorically, the yoke was used to describe
the Law which the Jewish youth undertook to bind to
himself in the *bar mitzvah* ceremony. It spoke of loyal
commitment. And here the carpenter of Nazareth who
had made many a yoke says in effect, 'My yokes fit well.
They do not rub your neck and shoulders. Come to me.
Get yoked up to me. Make that act of loyal obedience
to me like the *bar mitzvah*. And you will find a deep
peace and satisfaction in your life that you could never
find elsewhere. I have come for you. Come to me.'

There is a fascinating allusion here to the Book of
Wisdom. In Wisdom 'Put your necks under the yoke
of the law, and let your soul accept her burden. See,

I have worked but little and found much rest.' It is only an allusion and not a quotation, and many of his hearers might not pick it up. But if they did, its claim is as shattering as anything in this section. It is saying that what the Law was to Israel, Jesus is to the citizens of the kingdom. This metaphor was not forgotten in the Church. The *Didache* calls Christ's commandments 'the yoke of the law'. His yoke is gentle, not in the sense that it is less demanding than Judaism. In some ways it is more demanding. But it is the yoke of love, not of duty. It is the response of the liberated, not of the obligated. And that makes all the difference.

Reflection

What sort of things cause you to feel 'weary and burdened'? How does feeling this way affect your relationships, both with other people and with God? How does it affect the way you feel about yourself? Write down your thoughts.

Slowly read the Bible passage again, and hear Jesus' words as addressed personally to you. In his invitation, there is something to take, something to learn, and something to find: what are they? What is your response? Give yourself time to allow thoughts and feelings to surface. You may feel comforted by the offer of rest, or you may feel let down by it, or angry, thinking that none of it seems to apply to you. Don't try to analyse your feelings now, but write them down, however confused or weary they may be, and then bring them before God in honest prayer.

27

Living in the Bible

Reading: John 20:30–31

Jesus did many other miraculous signs in the presence of his disciples, which are not recorded in this book. But these are written that you may believe that Jesus is the Christ, the Son of God, and that by believing you may have life in his name.

If we are persuaded that the Scriptures do indeed come to us with the stamp of God's authority, that will have a number of implications for our evangelistic ministry.

We will not be embarrassed about opening the Scriptures. We will turn to them with the same naturalness with which we would turn to any other book. The Bible is the world's best-seller, but it is an unread best-seller. People are ignorant of its contents. And there need be no hint of Bible-thumping if we turn to its pages and show people what it actually says. That is, in any discipline, a thoroughly reputable procedure: get back to the primary sources.

We will take any opportunities to lend the Scriptures.

The loan or gift of an attractively presented Gospel in a modern translation is often extremely influential in the reader's life. I recall the story of Tikichi Ishii, a Second World War criminal of almost unmatched cruelty, who was awaiting execution in his cell. With fiendish brutality this Japanese guard had murdered men, women and children, and had revelled in it. Two Canadian women visited him in his cell, and told him of the salvation which Christ had achieved even for such as he. He glared at them, cursing, and they went away without apparently having achieved anything. But they left him a New Testament. He began to read it during the long hours of enforced solitude. He was fascinated by the person of Jesus, who was tortured so brutally, but without a word of resentment. Rather, he had prayed for his tormenters, 'Father, forgive them; for they know not what they do' (Luke 23:34).

Ishii said later, 'I stopped. I could not go on. I was stabbed to the heart, as by a five-inch nail. Was it the love of Christ? Was it his compassion? I do not know what it was. I only know that I believed, and the hardness of my heart was changed.' And when the executioner came to Ishii he found not the hardened brute he had anticipated, but a smiling, radiant man whose remaining days in that prison had been utterly transformed by the new life he had found in Christ. We may have confidence in lending the Scriptures to others. It is a quiet but very powerful means of evangelism.

Evangelists should also be prepared to challenge people with the Scriptures. Not only in public preaching, but also in personal conversation. Often I have said to an enquirer with whom I have been talking, 'Here is a copy of St John's Gospel. It tells us that it was written to bring people like you to the intellectual belief that Jesus was the Son of God, and to the experience of a new life through him. Why not read it with an open mind, prepared to commit yourself to the cause of Christ if, and only if, you are convinced? Pray as you read, "O God, if you are real (and I am not sure you are), show me what is true in this account, and I promise that if I am persuaded, I will entrust my life to Christ."' Often they return to tell me that the experiment has had a powerful effect on them. They have read it with an open mind. They have been convinced. And they have begun the life of Christian discipleship.

Most of all, those who are seeking to share the good news need to trust the Scriptures. They have a power our words do not. Any experienced minister will have known occasions when some verse of Scripture read in a lesson has pierced to the very heart of a hearer, or when a word of Scripture which he passed over lightly in his address has totally grabbed the attention of someone in the congregation, closing their mind and ears to all else, and has subsequently made a real change in the direction of that person's life. There are times when preachers who are exposing people to the message of the Bible can almost stand outside themselves and watch the divine chemistry at work. It is so obviously not the work of the preachers themselves. One person will be moved to tears by the address: the next person will be looking at their watch, waiting for the sermon to stop!

Reflection

Write down five words or phrases to describe your attitude to the Bible. How has it changed or developed over the years? How important is it to you? How do you feel when a non-believer sees it on your shelf? Why?

How would you describe what the Bible is, to someone who knew nothing about it?

What part does the Bible play in the working out of your relationship with the living Christ?

We have such easy access to the Bible in this country that many of us tend to take it for granted. We hear it read so often in church, that we may forget the immense power it can have on those who do not know Christ, as it did on Tikichi Ishii. Ask God's forgiveness for the times you have treated the Bible carelessly or lightly. Ask him to deepen your love for the Bible and to open your heart and mind to hear him speak through its pages. Ask him too if there is anyone to whom he would like you to offer a Bible, or with whom he would like you to talk about it, this week.

28

Taking Communion

Reading: Matthew 26:20–29

When evening came, Jesus was reclining at the table with the Twelve. And while they were eating, he said, 'I tell you the truth, one of you will betray me.'

They were very sad and began to say to him one after the other, 'Surely not I, Lord?'

Jesus replied, 'The one who has dipped his hand into the bowl with me will betray me. The Son of Man will go just as it is written about him. But woe to that man who betrays the Son of Man! It would be better for him if he had not been born.'

Then Judas, the one who would betray him, said, 'Surely not I, Rabbi?'

Jesus answered, 'Yes, it is you.'

While they were eating, Jesus took bread, gave thanks and broke it, and gave it to his disciples, saying, 'Take and eat; this is my body.'

Then he took the cup, gave thanks and offered it to them, saying, 'Drink from it, all of you.

'This is my blood of the covenant, which is poured out for many for the forgiveness of sins. I tell you, I will not drink of this fruit of the vine from now on until that day when I drink it anew with you in my Father's kingdom.'

When they had sung a hymn, they went out to the Mount of Olives.

At the heart of Christian fellowship lies the Holy Communion, Eucharist, Mass, Lord's Supper – call it what you will. Incidentally, each of those names stresses one side of the central act of Christian devotion. 'Holy Communion' reminds us that we come there in order to deepen our communion and fellowship with a holy God and with other members of his family. 'Eucharist' means 'thanksgiving' and warms our hearts with gratitude for all Christ has done to bring us into the family. 'Mass' probably means either 'meal' or 'dismissal' of those who are not baptised into Christ – this intimate family meal is for believing members of the family and none others. And 'Lord's Supper' reminds us who is the host and celebrant at that meal, Jesus himself, the one who inaugurated it at the last supper he had with his disciples on earth.

We come then, looking back to the cross; the cross he was going to when he had that supper with them. He told them, as he broke the bread, that his body would be broken for them; he told them, as he distributed the cup, that his blood would be shed for them. It happened the very next day. How we need to go back time and again to Calvary with grateful hearts in order to reappropriate the forgiveness Christ won for us there! That is where our adoption certificate into the family was issued, where our citizen rights in the new society were secured, at such tremendous cost. The Communion awakens us afresh to the awfulness of sin, the greatness of his sacrifice and the wonder of our forgiveness.

We should also approach the Communion with a good long look at our own lives, in the light of that love of Christ's. How far do we come short of his considerateness, love, purity and honesty? Now is the time to search our consciences, get right with him, and as we stretch out our empty hands for the bread and the wine, symbols of his self-giving, to remember that we are indeed empty in ourselves; we deserve no good thing from God. We come simply by right of his generous free invitation to receive what he offers us – himself.

A third side to the Holy Communion is this. The early Christians knew that 'the Lord is at hand'. It was no festival in honour of a dead Jesus, but a meal of companionship with a risen Lord. So thank him that he is alive, that he is at work in you and the rest of the community of the resurrection, as the Church might well be called. That is something to rejoice about.

Make a point, too, of looking around you. That old lady, that bluff shop-keeper, that lanky youth, that friendly bus-driver – you all belong together in the Lord's family. You all kneel or sit together to receive the bread and wine, the sacred emblems of his body and his blood given without distinction for you all. No place for pride before such self-giving love, is there? No need to have any chip on the shoulder! No excuse for keeping up a feud with any other member of the same family. You are all on a par: fellow-sinners, fellow-heirs of the same kingdom and fellow-guests at the same table.

And spare a thought for the future God has for his new society. It may not bring in Utopia on earth. God never said it would. But each Lord's Supper should have a touch of the future glory about it. It should remind us of the Marriage Supper of the Lamb (as the Book of Revelation picturesquely calls it), the final consummation in joyous harmony of God's plan for all his people. '*Maranatha!*' cried the earliest Christians in their native Aramaic, when they sat at the Lord's Table. 'O, Lord, come!' It is as if they said, 'Lord, you have come to this world, and lived and died for us. You have set us in this new society. We see many marks of your presence and of your renewing work. But, Lord, there's such a long way to go. Hasten the day when you wind up your plans for this world, and bring us all to the family table in heaven.' No escapism, there, you will notice. But just a foretaste of the future glory to give us perspective in our daily work, and the determination to be the best for him on earth.

Make room, then, for informal fellowship at home and at work; make room for meeting other Christians, especially on Sunday; make room for services of other kinds; but, whatever you do, do not neglect Holy Communion. It is the seal of your pardon, the food for your Christian life, the bond of your fellowship and the foretaste of heaven.

Reflection

What does Holy Communion mean to you? Why is it important (or not important) for you to receive it? What feelings do you have about it – or have you received it so often that you tend to take it for granted, and don't think or feel much about it at all? As you think now, write down your thoughts and pray for a fresh understanding of the significance of this holy meal.

How would you explain what Holy Communion is to a non-believer?

29

Encountering Christ

Reading: Philippians 3:8–11

I consider everything a loss compared to the surpassing greatness of knowing Christ Jesus my Lord, for whose sake I have lost all things. I consider them rubbish, that I may gain Christ and be found in him, not having a righteousness of my own that comes from the law, but that which is through faith in Christ – the righteousness that comes from God and is by faith. I want to know Christ and the power of his resurrection and the fellowship of sharing in his sufferings, becoming like him in his death, and so, somehow, to attain to the resurrection from the dead.

This is how a university teacher in computing science has described to me her appreciation of the encounter with Christ that has changed her life:

The best thing that has ever happened to me was the dawning awareness that Jesus Christ was not just a historic figure; a good man dead and gone. Mysterious though it seems, he is the Son of God, who died on behalf of all, rose from the dead, and now offers life to any who dares to trust him. I have taken this step of faith. I know I am alive. Jesus has brought strong and consistent meaning to my life. More than anything in the world I want to live my life for him. I want him to be my Number One. Walking with Jesus through life is the most liberating of all possible relationships. Jesus understands me better than I can ever hope to understand myself. Gradually he is releasing me from my 'hang-ups' and enabling me to discover and to become the person he wants me to be. His capacity for loving and forgiving is endless. He forgives me even when I cannot forgive myself. Nothing can ever separate him from me, so I am never alone.

If Jesus were not alive I could not be writing as I am. His love for me brings a security and hope in this unstable and changing world. Living for him, motivated and helped by his Spirit within, is the biggest challenge anyone could be given. Perhaps the words of Dom Julian best express what I feel most deeply:

> *If everything is lost, thanks be to God.*
> *If I must see it go, watch it go,*
> *Watch it fade away, die,*
> *Thanks be to God that he is all I have*
> *And if I have him not, I have nothing at all.*

This is the sort of testimony that many of our contemporaries bear to Jesus Christ. They speak of what they actually know from their own experience of Jesus.

That may not seem very satisfactory. It might be tidier if it were possible to prove the matter one way or the other. But life is not like that. It simply is not possible to put into words an experience which has changed your life, let alone to prove it. That is what a Ghanaian friend of mine was struggling to say when he wrote: 'I know Jesus lives, because I meet him every day, and share fellowship with him. Fellowship can only exist between people who are *living*. I think that the truth that Jesus lives is something that one can experience rather than describe.'

That is true enough. And it is borne out by this story a Czechoslovak theologian told me. A Russian lecturer, a member of the Communist party, was addressing a packed audience on the subject of the resurrection of Jesus Christ. He spoke at considerable length, seeking to discredit it. At the end, an Orthodox priest rose and asked if he might reply. He was warned that he could have only five minutes. 'Five seconds is all I shall need' was his reply. He turned to the audience, and gave the delightful Easter greeting, characteristic of the Eastern church. '*Christos anestē*,' he cried, 'Christ is risen.' Back with a deafening roar came the traditional reply from the crowded hall, '*Alethōs anestē*', 'Truly he is risen.'

That is the essence of the Christian witness down the centuries. It has not changed since some of the disciples encountered Jesus on the first Easter Day.

The heart of the matter for the Christian is this: Jesus did not merely rise, he is alive. Alive and ready to be met by men, women or children who are willing to share their lives with him.

That is not the common image of Christianity. God forgive us, we have smothered the risen Christ in denominationalism, ecclesiasticism, respectability, moralism and goodness knows what else. But that is the heart of authentic Christianity.

Christians are the 'community of the resurrection'. They are like iron filings attracted to and adhering to the magnetic person of Jesus Christ, risen from the dead.

It is impossible to do justice to the evidence for the resurrection unless you take into account this worldwide testimony from believers great and small that Jesus is not a dead hero, but a living Lord.

Reflection

How would you describe your own encounter with Christ?

In what ways do you find that 'walking with Jesus through life is the most liberating of all possible relationships'?

For further study
In what ways have you found that the Church has 'smothered the risen Christ' and been distracted from the heart of authentic Christianity? What could you do to help to change this?

30

Lighting up the darkness

Reading: John 1:1–14

In the beginning was the Word, and the Word was with God, and the Word was God. He was with God in the beginning.

Through him all things were made; without him nothing was made that has been made. In him was life, and that life was the light of men. The light shines in the darkness, but the darkness has not understood it.

There came a man who was sent from God; his name was John. He came as a witness to testify concerning that light, so that through him all men might believe. He himself was not the light; he came only as a witness to the light. The true light that gives light to every man was coming into the world.

He was in the world, and though the world was made through him, the world did not recognise him. He came to that which was his own, but his own did not receive him. Yet to all who received him, to those who believed in his name, he gave the right to become children of God – children born not of natural descent, nor of human decision or a husband's will, but born of God.

The Word became flesh and lived for a while among us. We have seen his glory, the glory of the one and only [Son], who came from the Father, full of grace and truth.

John has no doubt who Jesus is. And he expresses it in
terms which would have been familiar to his readers
in the first century. 'The Word' was used as much in
common language then as 'quantum' is today. It was
the term used for the ultimate colleague of God in
creation: the Jews used it of the divine 'wisdom'. And
John wasn't only writing to Jews. He was writing to Greeks
as well. For them the logos, or the word, was the rational
power of God which created the whole universe and kept
everything going.

John takes this well-known concept of the Word and
boldly identifies it with Jesus. And how appropriate it is!
Just as I cannot know what is in your mind unless you
clothe it in 'word', so we cannot know what is in the mind
of God unless he does the same. John proclaims that this
is precisely what God has done. Jesus reveals the God we
cannot see as closely as your words reveal the thoughts I
could not grasp. 'The Word became flesh' – God's Word.
That is who Jesus is.

Look at what John claims for the Word. He maintains
first and foremost that the Word is God. Not a great
teacher, not a wonder worker, but God, no less. And in
the verses that follow he fills out that claim.

The Word was the agent in creation. He shared with the
Father in the creation of the world. St John is certain that
Jesus is no great guru, but God incarnate.

The Word is, moreover, 'the life'. The life-giving principle throughout nature, and supremely in human beings,
is an aspect of Jesus. All life derives from him.

The Word is 'the light of men', and Jesus said, 'I am
the light of the world.' The person of Jesus attracts men

and women the world over who are open to goodness. He *is* the light. His teaching is light. His lifestyle is light. His death and resurrection are a veritable beacon. Jesus is 'the light of men' and to reject him is to walk in darkness. That is not to deny that there are many candles in this dark world. Socrates was a candle. Gandhi was a candle. But Jesus is no candle. He is the sun, shining in its strength.

Does this seem an exaggeration? John is aware of that objection, too, and so he says, 'The light shines in darkness but the darkness has not understood it.' There's a sturdy realism here: John knows that 'darkness' is a frank description of our society. And the darkness has never understood Jesus of Nazareth, the Light of the world. Actually a more probable translation of the Greek would be 'the darkness has never extinguished' the Light. And manifestly, that is the case.

Jesus, the life of humankind, the light of the world, is no bland figure to whom all are polite. He has always attracted a lot of opposition from the forces of darkness. 'The world did not recognise him' – and that is still the case. He came to the world he had made, and his very own people did not want to know. There is something in human beings that is intrinsically opposed to the goodness and the ultimate claims that reside in Jesus of Nazareth.

Nevertheless the shocking truth stands firm. It is he, and he alone, who can gain entrance for us into the Royal Family, the family of God. It is, John tells us, only those who 'receive' Jesus and 'believe in' him who are welcomed by his heavenly Father. It is not a matter of trying hard. It is not a matter of going to church. It is a matter of recognising who Jesus is, and surrendering our lives to him. For he alone is the divine adoption agency. He is the way into the family of God.

And when we do respond to him in adoring love, as St John and his friends had done, we discover glory, 'the glory of the One and Only . . . full of grace and truth'. We see in Jesus the perfect reflection of the unutterable beauty of God. For that is what he is. 'No one has ever seen God,' John reminds us, 'but God the One and Only, who is at the Father's side, has made him known.'

That is what makes Jesus so special. That is what sets him apart from all the great religious teachers down the ages. He makes God known, without distortion: he embodies God.

And yet that is a dangerous half truth. If he were simply God, he could not truly be one of us, could not fully understand us. But John is quick to guard against that misconception. 'The Word became flesh,' he tells us. 'The Word', the highest concept in Judaism, chose to become flesh – one of us. He was really God, and really human. That is the mystery of the person of Jesus. We must never lose grasp of either terminal: through them flows the electricity of authentic Christianity. Almost all heresies begin with some interpretation of the person of Jesus. We shall never plumb the mystery of what it means to be both divine and human; but if we hold firm to both assertions we shall not go far astray on the central truth of Christianity, the incarnation.

Reflection

'There are many candles in this dark world . . . But Jesus is no candle. He is the sun, shining in its strength.' Who have been the 'candles' for you personally? People who have helped you to faith, perhaps, or who have been there for you in times of crisis? Thank God for them now, and if you have never really been able to thank the people themselves, think about sending them a card, or a bunch of flowers, to say how much you appreciate them.

*   *   *

How has Jesus been 'the sun shining in its strength' in your life? Try to think of specific instances and thank him for them.

In what ways do you want Jesus to be the light of your life now and in your future? If there is a particular sense at the moment in which you feel in darkness – you may be confused about a decision that you have to make, or you may be experiencing depression, grief, or loneliness – ask Christ to shine gently but powerfully into your darkness and to help you forward.

Acknowledgments

All Bible readings are from the Holy Bible, New International Version, © 1973, 1978, 1984 by International Bible Society, 1980 edition, 1987 impression, published by Hodder & Stoughton.
Book extracts are as follows:
Chapters 1, 7, 9, 11, 12, 20, 24, 27 from *Evangelism Through the Local Church* by Michael Green, © 1990, published by Hodder & Stoughton Ltd.
Chapters 2, 5, 13, 18, 19, 22 from *The Empty Cross of Jesus* by Michael Green, © 1984, published by Hodder & Stoughton Ltd.
Chapters 3, 15 from *You Must Be Joking* by Michael Green, © 1976, published by Hodder & Stoughton Ltd.
Chapters 4, 10, 16, 25, 26 from *Matthew For Today* by Michael Green, © 1988, published by Hodder & Stoughton Ltd.
Chapter 17 from *Acts For Today* by Michael Green, © 1993, published by Hodder & Stoughton Ltd.
Chapter 6 from *I Believe in the Holy Spirit* by Michael Green, © 1975, published by Hodder & Stoughton Ltd.
Chapter 8 from *Who Is This Jesus?* by Michael Green, © 1990, published by Hodder & Stoughton Ltd.
Chapter 14 from *Freed to Serve* by Michael Green, © 1983, published by Hodder & Stoughton Ltd.
Chapters 21, 28 from *New Life, New Lifestyle* by Michael Green, © 1973, published by Hodder & Stoughton Ltd.
Chapter 23 from *I Believe in Satan's Downfall* by Michael Green, © 1981, published by Hodder & Stoughton Ltd.
Chapter 29 from *The Day Death Died* by Michael Green, © 1982, published by Inter-Varsity Press.
Chapter 30 from *Good News and How to Share It* by Michael Green, © 1993, published by The Bible Reading Fellowship.